Letters on the Spanish Inquisition
by Joseph Marie Comte De Maistre

Copyright © 2019 by HardPress

Address:
HardPress
8345 NW 66TH ST #2561
MIAMI FL 33166-2626
USA
Email: info@hardpress.net

5480
22.15

SPANISH INQUISITION.

C549.22.15

Harvard College Library

FROM THE FUND BEQUEATHED BY
Archibald Cary Coolidge
Class of 1887
PROFESSOR OF HISTORY
1908-1928
DIRECTOR OF THE UNIVERSITY LIBRARY
1910-1928

LETTERS

ON THE

SPANISH INQUISITION:

A RARE WORK,

AND

THE BEST WHICH HAS EVER APPEARED ON THE SUBJECT.

BY

M. LE COMTE JOSEPH LE MAISTRE.

TRANSLATED FROM THE FRENCH,

WITH A

PREFACE, ADDITIONAL NOTES AND ILLUSTRATIONS,

BY

T. J. O'FLAHERTY, S. E. C.

BOSTON:
PATRICK DONAHOE, CATHOLIC BOOKSELLER.

1843.

Entered according to Act of Congress, in the year 1843, by
PATRICK DONAHOE,
In the Clerk's Office of the District Court of Massachusetts.

TO THE MEMORY OF
CARDINAL CHEVERUS,
FIRST CATHOLIC BISHOP OF BOSTON

MASSACHUSETTS,

WHOSE NOBLE QUALITIES OF HEAD AND HEART REFLECTED LUSTRE ON EUROPE AND AMERICA;

ALSO,

TO THE MEMORY OF

THE RIGHT REV. JOHN ENGLAND,

FIRST CATHOLIC BISHOP OF CHARLESTON,

SOUTH CAROLINA,

THE GOOD AND GREAT,

WHOSE BRILLIANT POWERS,

AS SCHOLAR, CONTROVERSIALIST, ORATOR, AND DIVINE,

WILL EVER BE HELD IN MERITED ADMIRATION BY THE CIVILIZED WORLD,

THIS STEREOTYPE EDITION

OF

LETTERS ON THE INQUISITION OF SPAIN

IS MOST RESPECTFULLY AND HUMBLY

𝔈𝔫𝔰𝔠𝔯𝔦𝔟𝔢𝔡,

BY THE TRANSLATOR,

THOMAS J. O'FLAHERTY,

CATHOLIC PASTOR OF SALEM,

MASSACHUSETTS.

PREFACE.

At the memorable and melancholy period of the misnamed *reformation*, every expedient that human ingenuity could devise, or depravity invent, was brought into formidable action against the institutions of society and the religion of Heaven. Rebellion struck at, and endeavored to annihilate, whatever the wisdom of time had protected, morality cherished, patriotism and virtue held dear. A blasphemous effort had been made to blow up "the rock" upon which Jesus Christ had built his Holy Church.

Innovation, the daring offspring of selfishness and pride, flung a worse than Gothic gloom over an immense portion of the European mind, and, coöperating with the prince of darkness, cruelly sought to establish the empire of libertinism by emancipating the tyrannic passions of the human heart from the mild and light yoke of the cross.

Among the licentious ringleaders of this innovation, a Luther of Germany, a Calvin of France, and a Henry VIII. of England, stand *preëminent;* — all *reformers!* all *pious* and "honorable men"! Luther, in all the sensitiveness of a *scrupulous* conscience, fulminated his *reforming* abuses at the INDULGENCES of the Catholic Church; while, upon the plea of "the impossibility of keeping God's commandments, and the futility, nay, *injuriousness,* of GOOD

WORKS to a Christian soul," he allows *himself* an INDULGENCE to violate his solemn *moral* and *religious* vows of celibacy and Christian self-denial, contrary to what he read in the twenty-third chapter twenty-first verse of Deuteronomy; and long before he had made them of *his own free will and accord*, — " When thou hast *made a vow* to the Lord thy God, thou shalt *not delay to pay it*; because the Lord thy God *will require it*: and if thou *delay*, it shall be *imputed to thee as a sin*"!! He next became guilty of the double crime of sacrilege, by *seducing*, and afterwards *acting the part of a husband* to CATHARINE BOREN, to whom he granted an INDULGENCE; and who had also solemnly consecrated herself to God, for the express purpose of leading a life of Christian seclusion, celibacy, purity, and piety!*

This he had done, contrary to a statute of Heaven, —

---

* The supposed stumbling-block to the disorganizing broachers of a spurious *reformation*, was the doctrine of the Catholic Church in relation to INDULGENCES! It was made to serve those " who strained out gnats, and swallowed camels," as a justification of their departure from the " one faith," and the " one fold," of the Shepherd of eternal life!

As there is scarcely a tenet of the divine religion of the Savior which has been more scandalously misrepresented by Protestant parsons and Protestant historians, (among whom we may, consistently with the *principles* of the *reformation*, rank the prejudiced infidel Hume — see Cobbett's valuable " History of the Reformation,") it may not be amiss to state here what the Catholic Church has EVER meant by the term INDULGENCE.

Our adorable Savior declared to his apostles that ALL POWER *was given him in heaven and on earth*. He also said, *As the* FATHER *hath sent me, I also send you*. (He uses the word *Father* in reference to his *humanity*; for, with regard to the Deity, "THE WORD WAS GOD;" the FATHER and the SON were ONE in divine nature and essence.) " And when He had said this, He breathed on them; and He said to them, RECEIVE YE THE HOLY GHOST: *whose sins you shall forgive*, they are forgiven them; and *whose sins you shall retain*, they are retained." (See St. John, chap. 20.) Here we see a judiciary power immediately conferred upon the

"Thou shalt not commit adultery,"— and in opposition to the profitable advice of St. Paul (as recorded in his First apostles, and an implied necessity, on their part, to exercise it, as well as upon the part of the laity, *when truly sorry for sin, and determined thenceforth to avoid evil, and do good,* to avail themselves of its advantages; for, otherwise, such faculties, if not brought into action, would defeat the very intention and object of the God of wisdom, " the Author of every good and perfect gift." CONFESSION OF SINS, therefore, to the apostles of the new law, the true priests of the Holy Catholic Church, and their legitimate successors, was hereby established by our divine Redeemer, for all those who would " hear the Church," for all those who would aspire to salvation, according to the plan designed by the great Messiah. That He, who is " the Alpha and Omega of all things," *who is before Abraham was,* and who came to *fulfil,* not to destroy, the law, had established the *confession of sins,* even under the Mosaic dispensation, is proved from the BOOK OF NUMBERS, chap. 5, v. 6, 7: " When a man or woman shall have committed any of all the sins that men are wont to commit, and by negligence shall have transgressed the commandment of the Lord, and offended, they shall *confess their sin,* and *restore the principal itself,* and the fifth part over and above, to him against whom they have sinned." Such, then, was the nature of confession and satisfaction in ancient times, — a type of what our Savior had instituted in the days of the apostles. Now, as sin is a transgression of the law of God, in thought, word, or deed, or omission of duty, and as man may become guilty, either by not doing what he ought, or doing what he ought not, and as there are various degrees of sin, owing to the nature and circumstances of the case, there ought to be different degrees of punishment, adapted to the nature and circumstances of the offence. Upon that principle, the penal laws of the civilized world are, or at least should be, founded. Hence Almighty God requires of all who *have the opportunity* of approaching the tribunal of penance; *after being duly sorry for sin, and making a firm purpose of amendment,* to submit to the decisions of that tribunal, and formally receive the virtue of the Holy Ghost, and of the apostolic commission, " Whatsoever sins you loose upon earth, shall be loosed also in heaven." It is not the business of man to ask *why* the Savior of the world laid such an injunction upon him, for when God speaks, man *should* obey. THE RELAXATION OR FORGIVENESS OF THE TEMPORAL PUNISHMENT DUE TO SIN, AFTER THE ETERNAL PUNISHMENT HAS BEEN REMITTED IN THE SACRAMENT OF PENANCE, IS WHAT HAS EVER BEEN CALLED *AN INDULGENCE* BY THE ONE HOLY ROMAN CATHOLIC AND APOSTOLIC CHURCH. How cruel, how iniquitous, therefore, must it be for the adversaries of truth, among whom was the hireling infidel,

Epistle to the Corinthians, chap. 7, verses 32, 33,) which is strictly appropriate to the *true priests* of the true

---

HUME, to state that an INDULGENCE, in our divine religion, signifies " A PERMISSION TO COMMIT ANY OR EVERY SIN "!!!

That a temporal punishment awaits the penitent even *after* the remission of the eternal penalty, strange as it may appear to Protestants, is satisfactorily proved by Scripture. We read in the BOOK OF NUMBERS, that the Lord, after he had pardoned the Israelites for their ungrateful and iniquitous murmuring, had debarred them from the *Promised Land*, on account of that sin. We find that, after the royal David had repented of his adulterous intercourse, and was assured by the prophet Nathan, on the part of God, that the sin was forgiven, a *temporal* punishment, (*the death of the illicit offspring*,) as predicted by the man of God, had actually followed. So much for the *temporal* punishment. That this can be *moderated*, or *forgiven*, is proved by St. Paul's conduct towards the incestuous Corinthian, whose body had been delivered over to Satan, but who, after his penitential tears, and true amendment of life, had been freed by that great apostle, " in the person of Christ." from that awful calamity. In a word, from the days of the apostles down to the present period, the Catholic Church, by virtue of the power which Christ gave her, has granted the relaxation of this temporal punishment, or THIS INDULGENCE, whenever the spiritual good of the penitent required it, and when there existed a well-grounded apprehension that a rigorous penance would prove prejudicial to him. Hence what the apostle says to the Corinthians in relation to that sorrowing sinner, the Church observes to her pastors, in all penitential cases, " You should rather pardon and comfort him, lest perhaps such a one be swallowed up with overmuch sorrow."

An INDULGENCE, it must be remembered, never did, never was intended to, forgive or mitigate the *eternal* punishment of sin, or its *natural* consequences, such as all the moral and physical evils entailed upon the world by original sin. Neither was it ever meant by our Savior, or his Church, to shield a culprit from the salutary severity of the civil law. It is altogether restricted to spiritual penalties required by divine justice, *after* the sinner is acquitted of the crimes for which he stood indicted by the supreme court of Heaven, — penalties which a true priest, a judicial representative of the Church, " in the person of Christ," is vested by virtue of his commission, " Whatever you shall bind or loose upon earth shall be bound or loosed in heaven," to relax or forgive.

What was there, in all this scriptural usage and apostolic precedent, that could have *justified* Luther in railing at the immaculate spouse, and rending the seamless garb of Christ? Upon *such* grounds did he tear himself from the bosom of Unity, call himself a *reformer*, and involve Germany in heresy, infidelity, horror, and blood. — *Translator.*

Church: "But I would have you to be without solicitude. He that is without a wife, is solicitous for the things that belong to the Lord, how he may please God. But he that is with a wife, is solicitous for the things of the world, how he may please his wife; and he is divided." To secure the secular power to his cause, as well as to illustrate the *evangelical* character of the *reformation*, he transmitted an INDULGENCE to Philip, the landgrave of Hesse, to keep *two wives* at the same time.

The unfortunate Calvin, branded between the shoulders for a crime of nameless turpitude at Noyon, in Picardy, was exiled from France, and sought refuge at Geneva, in Switzerland.* Actuated by the most ferocious hatred to his native country, her institutions and religion, he vomits forth, in all the wickedness of a desperado, the most *wanton* invectives against the laws and religion of the Catholic world. He blasphemously attacks incarnate Deity, publicly maintains that He died in despair upon the cross, and makes God to be the author of sin! A registered and criminal outlaw, he, too, conceived the project of effecting *a reformation* in the moral, religious world! He, *of course*,

---

* "Inspiciuntur etiam adhuc hodie civitatis Noviodunensis in Picardia, scrinia et rerum gestarum monumenta: in illis adhuc hodie legitur Joannem hunc Calvinum sodomice convictum, ex episcopi et magistratus indulgentia, solo stigmate in tergo notatum, urbe excessisse; nec ejus familiæ honestissimi viri, adhuc superstites, impetrare hactenus potuerunt, ut hujus facti memoria, quæ toti familiæ notam aliquam inurit, e civicis illis monumentis ac scriniis eraderetur." (a) Moreover, the Lutherans of Germany speak of it as a fact: "De Calvini variis flagitiis et sodomiticis libidinibus, ob quas stigma Joannis Calvini dorso impressum fuit a magistratu, sub quo vixit." (b)

(a) *Promptuar. Catholic.* pars. 32, p. 133.
(b) Conrad. Schlussemb, *Calvin. Theolog.* lib. ii. ii. fol. 72. — *Translator.*

protested against the ancient Church, although the "Prince of Peace," who was "the way, the truth, and the life," had unequivocally declared that He *would* be with His Church all days, even to the end of time; although *she was the pillar and ground of truth;* although He had *confirmed* her in *all truth,* and thrown around her the consoling assurance that "the gates of hell should never prevail against her." With such *convictions* on his mind, and after so promising a preparation in his native place, Calvin made his *debut* by burning SERVETUS, a Spanish physician and Socinian, at the stake, and also caused BRUET, an unfortunate Frenchman, to be put to death, because they would not agree with him in *his "private interpretation,"* and *"orthodox"* decisions of the Bible!*

---

* The disciples of John Calvin, not content with bearing the name of Calvinists, (perhaps it is because they are ashamed of their *religious* father,) have absurdly assumed the name of "*Orthodox* Christians." "*Risum teneatis, amici?*" We have ever understood, from the Greek and ecclesiastical acceptation of the word *orthodoxy,* that it signified *sound opinions and apostolic doctrine.* Where was the doctrine of John Calvin in the days of the apostles, who, before their departure from Jerusalem to "teach all nations," drew up a constitution of faith which is known by the name of "THE APOSTLES' CREED"? Is not the expression, "I BELIEVE IN THE HOLY CATHOLIC CHURCH," found in that very creed? Will Calvinists say that their religion was always in "the Bible"? Will not the Ranters, and Quakers, and Shakers, and Socinians, say the same? What does it prove? Was not Christianity, was not "the Holy Catholic Church," planted and propagated long before the New Testament was heard of? Hence the necessity of sectarians admitting a living and unerring authority, and *not* the dead letter exclusively; hence the indispensable duty of "hearing THE CHURCH," under penalty of being considered "as the heathen and publican." As the pseudo-reformation *churches* came into the world fifteen hundred years too late, it is evident that "the Church," to which our Savior alluded, was that which He erected upon St. Peter's faith, and which the apostles designated, in their constitution and council, by the name of "the Holy Catholic Church." So much for *Calvinistic Orthodoxy.* — *Translator.*

Henry VIII. of England, because the pope of Rome would not sanction a divorce between him and his faithful, virtuous queen, Catharine of Arragon, and for having so far prevented "that incestuous, that adulterous beast" from giving full scope to his inordinate passions, renounced the authority and the religion of the Catholic Church, which had, for the preceding fifteen centuries, shed the odor of sanctity and of apostolic morality throughout all the nations of the earth. He also assumes and discharges the office of a *reformer* in morals and religion! How he acted his part, the blood-stained page of history most painfully records. Murder, rapine, and lust, were the favorite deities of his new-fangled religion.

Thus lustful power, prejudice, and passion, entered into an unholy alliance against the Church of Christ at the commencement of the sixteenth century; and, under the false colors of a piratical, Pharisaical reformation, with all the exterminating fury of pagan persecution, and the ferocious and libidinous rankness of Mahometanism, fought its way with fire and sword into the Christian world, profaned the sanctuaries of religion, prostituted virtue, butchered patriotism and piety, annihilated order and law, and established their iniquitous empire upon the ruins of nature and revelation. The seeds of the misnamed REFORMATION, as sown by the base apostate Luther, had produced a thirty years' war in Germany, which thus became an immense Golgotha; and desolation and death alternately presented the tragic scene to the tear-burnt eyes of humanity. Catholic Switzerland, France, and the Netherlands, were immolated upon the altar of remorseless Calvinism. Once happy England, enlightened, hospitable, Catholic Ireland, and the once Catholic Scotland, were converted into one vast "field of blood;" were buried under *a red sea* by royal tyranny, anti-Christian murder. Liberty was in ruins. Catholicity was seen retreating to an apostolic clime, or, under the guidance of the cross, speeding, on the wings of martyrdom, its glorious flight to heaven.

Libertinism, thus enthroned on power, with the press and sword at command, selects an administration composed of an infamous coalition of corrupted hearts and perverted minds. Murder was legalized, and despotism adored. The tyrant's whim became the vassal's faith. Wicked slaves of lust, avarice, and power, swore allegiance to the *reformation* spirit, and proved it, whenever practicable, by the confiscation of the Catholic patriot's land, by the varied destruction of the Catholic freeman's life.

The venerable and divine Church of Christ was thenceforward called "the Babylon of iniquity"! The supreme pontiff, the visible head of the Church, and the regular apostolic successor of St. Peter, was vilified by the name of "ANTICHRIST"! Our holy religion was pronounced "superstitious, damnable, and idolatrous"! The venal press has since constantly labored and brought into the world the unmixed lies, vile slanders, and gross misrepresentations, of the enemies of truth, of the base apostates from the Apostles' Creed. The sword and fagot, the halter and rack, have been promiscuously employed to secure and *establish* them in the minds of the people, as so many "*orthodox*" tenets, and saving items of faith. From the proneness of man unto evil, and the confederation of Satan, the world, and the flesh, against the salutary austerities and self-denials of the Catholic Church ever since its foundation, we should not wonder that the *reformationary* disciples, notwithstanding their ephemeral, contradictory, and Protean creeds, would all unite and agree in the persecution and abuse of every thing Catholic.* In the blindness of passion, prejudice of education, or wilfulness of ignorance, they either cannot, or will not, draw a line of distinction between Catholic faith and Catholic discipline, between nominal and practical Catholics.

---

* When sects in religion are numerous, they are the cause of Atheism. — *Bacon.*

The dissensions that prevail among the multiplied sects that are come forth from the schools of Luther and Calvin, (he might have included Henry VIII.,) have been unfortunately but too favorable to the birth and progress of incredulity. — *Dr. Kett's Considerations on the Prophecies.*

It is a fact that, before the *reformation,* infidels were scarcely known in the world : it is a fact that they have come forth in swarms from its bosom. It was from the writings of Herbert, Hobbes, Bloum, Shaftesbury, Bolingbroke, and Boyle, that Voltaire and his party drew the objections and errors, which they have brought so generally into fashion, into the world. According to Diderot and D'Alembert, the first step that the untractable Catholic takes is to adopt the Protestant principle of *private judgment.* He establishes himself judge of his religion, leaves it, and joins the reform. Dissatisfied with the incoherent doctrines he now discovers, he passes on to the Socinians, whose inconsequences soon drive him into Deism ; still pursued by unexpected difficulties, he throws himself into universal doubt, where, still experiencing uneasiness, he at last resolves to take the last step, and proceeds to terminate the long chain of his errors in Atheism. Let us not forget that the first link of this fatal chain is attached to the fundamental maxim of *private judgment.* It is therefore historically correct, that the same principle that created Protestantism three centuries ago, has never ceased, since that time, to spin it out into a thousand different sects, and has concluded by covering Europe with that multitude of freethinkers who place it on the verge of ruin.

When sects beget infidelity, and by infidelity revolutions, it is plain that the political safety of the states will only be secured by a return to religious unity. (See *Discussion Amicale.*) — *Translator.*

If kings and subjects who profess the Catholic religion be guilty of immorality and crime, ought such delinquencies to be visited upon that religion, and upon all those who practically observe it? As well might the perfidy of an Arnold be attributed to the heroic and patriotic worthies, or the republican and glorious principles, of 1776. If Catholic kings, according to the soundest policy, had founded institutions for the preservation of order, morality, and religion, and had thereby realized so important and desirable an end, — if their Catholic successors acted upon and cherished the same course of policy when they saw neighboring nations, who either neglected, or scornèd to adopt it, a devoted prey to anarchy, infidelity, and outrage, — we would naturally ask, even in the event of a comparatively trivial abuse in the administration of such highly-useful institutions, would it be just to impute that abuse not only to the institutions themselves, but to the holy religion of the Catholic world? Such, however, is the shameful inconsistency, the censurable conduct, of the preachers, parsons, and Protestant historians, of a *false* reformation. How many such parsons, or hireling writers, could be found in the Christian world, had the Roman Catholic and apostolic Church permitted her clergy to marry, and altogether dispensed with the necessity of confession? Would there be one? No.

If Protestant parsons were allowed to continue with their wives and children, and to enjoy the same livings they do at present, by becoming Catholic converts, or priests, would there be a Protestant preacher in Christendom? Not one. We would fearlessly abide by the decisions of their conscience. What must be the feelings, the mental misery, of those whom a soul-killing policy, and the certainty of being *thrown out of bread*, prevent from declaring "the truth as it is in Jesus," and from publicly displaying the inextinguishable torch of the one Holy Catholic Church, the vestal light of salvation! No wonder, then, that the Church of Christ, whose faith and canonical injunctions are equally obligatory, and one and the same all over the world, should be *wantonly* impugned and cruelly slandered for her uncompromising consistency, stern justice, and rigid adherence to "the Spirit of truth" and apostolic usages, by those whose temporal interest it is to proselytize a virtuous community to their heartless, headless, and heretical creeds.

America, to a certain extent, may be considered the daughter of Protestant England, from whom she received her language, religion, and laws.

In her colonial childhood, she read the most unwarrantable misrepresentations of Catholic tenets and Catholic countries, in her class and text-books.

After she had brought forth an offspring, who were to become a band of heroes, and snap the links of the galling chain that fettered and disgraced her, she unfortunately, yet, as she believed, dutifully, instilled into their youthful minds those nursery tales, originally modelled by England into romances, and which were worked up into histories by the venal and profligate, the Protestant and infidel enemies of Catholicity, and, more recently, fashioned into and vended under the shape of silly and surfeiting *tracts*, under the imposing name of "*vital religion.*"

But the hour has come — America is alarmed — her luminous statesmen and patriots already behold the appalling strides which Bible and tract and *mock*-temperance societies are making for the aggrandizement of self, the amalgamation of church and state, the impoverishment of the nation, and the destruction of the national Constitution. Have tracts or pamphlets been ever purposely written in a certain quarter, and industriously circulated by certain *itinerant* agents at the South, to fire the minds of the black population, and spread desolation through that enlightened and magnanimous portion of our Union?*

These *terrorists* are manfully opposed by the unflinching and republican spirit of the Catholic clergy; and hence the horrid falsehoods which sectarian presses and pulpits deal out against those who have the courage to oppose and expose such iniquity. Hence the vituperation with which a weekly newspaper, called "THE JESUIT, OR CATHOLIC SENTINEL," in Boston, has been constantly assailed, for taking a stand in defence, and for the explanation, of that divine religion which has descended from Jesus Christ, through St. Peter, in unbroken succession for upwards of eighteen hundred years, and which, now committed to the pastoral charge of his holiness, Pope PIUS VIII., can never be stayed in its onward, luminous course, until, like the fiery chariot of Elias, it reach the glorious goal of heaven. Yes, that journal, like the Church whose tenets and morality it will ever defend, suffers the Pharisaical malice, shame-

---

* Yes, in Boston.

less obloquy, and bigoted ribaldry, of sectarianism to pass by it, "like the idle wind which it respects not."

In vain will heresy declaim against that Church; in vain will it assert that she, who was sanctified by Christ God, ever was, or can be, polluted with the crime of persecution.

The very supposition would brand falsehood upon the brow of God, or — what *is* the truth — must stamp indelible infamy upon the brazen front of heresy. It has been lyingly asserted, some short time since, by an individual who styled himself a *preacher*,* and was acknowledged as such by a Puritanic branch of the Calvinistic family, that the pope sent over his inquisitor-general to establish the Inquisition in this country!!! This stupid, unqualified lie went the rounds of the sectarian presses, and it showed how "*wise* the children of this world are in their generation"! Yes, the object of this Satanic invention and circulation was to frighten silly maidens, foolish old women, and ignorant old men, out of additional *ways and means* to support the *reformation* clergy, with their dear partners, and their precious little children, in indolence and ease; and to strengthen " the BIBLE AND TRACT FUND," — a system which, unless it be constantly watched by freemen, will be wielded as an Archimedean engine against the republican liberty and life of America. But what is this bugbear, *this raw head and bloody bones*, this INQUISITION, of which we hear so much?

Is it not an institution partly civil, partly ecclesiastical? It is. Has it not been wisely designed for the *protection* of the true faith? Most certainly. Has it not prevented the

---

* *Lyman* Beecher.

sacred landmarks of morality and Christianity in Spain from being swept away by the sanguinary Gulf-stream of Jewish and Mahometan cruelty? Undoubtedly. Has it not built around her an adamantine wall, which has enabled her to defy all the atrocities, wars, and infidel horrors, to which a false reformation had given birth, and which threatened to convulse the Christian universe? Most unquestionably. It was the work of self-defence, and *not* of persecution. In Spain, as well as in every other Catholic country, a man may entertain whatever religious or irreligious opinions he likes, however opposed they may be to the aged and uniform religion of the land; *but*, he *must* keep them to *himself;* for, the moment he begins to dogmatize and to preach up his *religious,* or rather *irreligious, experience,* and thereby endeavors to shake the civil laws, which rise out of the foundation of the true faith and established religion of the country, (a religion which is the offspring of Heaven, and, of course, incapable of being *"reformed"* by man, whether saint, or sage, or sinner,) he is brought before the tribunal; and if, in the course of *testimony*, it satisfactorily appears to the ecclesiastical department that his tenets are heretical, and their moral consequences therefore dangerous to the peace and harmony of the country, the clerical members of the institution, as citizens, friends of order, and Christians, are *ex officio* bound to report accordingly. They first strive to convince him by mild and friendly argument, by entreaty and prayer, of the unscriptural and vicious tendency of his tenets; if he retract, and promise never more to dogmatize, the matter rests; and he is at perfect liberty to leave, or remain in the country.

But should he unfortunately relapse, and if this can be proved upon *unexceptionable evidence*, he is arrested, as a *dangerous hypocrite and impenitent relapser*, by the tribunal. He is formally excommunicated from the body of the faithful, and his property is confiscated to the crown. When handed over to the secular powers, (for let it be remembered that the Inquisition never condemns a culprit to death, and that the signature of a clerical member of that body *never* has been seen on the death-warrant,) the criminal is then punished according to his offence and the established law of the realm.

Every free nation must have its own laws and courts; and power is necessary to their security. How absurd, then, is the objection which heretics, as well as all those who are unacquainted with the principles of sound government, and the nature of this inquisitorial court, bring forward against Spanish kings, for establishing such tribunals as equity and experience have recommended for the safety of national happiness! Truth must never compromise; otherwise it would change its nature and its name. The toleration of error, in religious concerns, would be its ruin. The Inquisition, therefore, being a protective law of the only religion of Spain, the introduction of religious error, or heresy, must be considered a species of counterfeit, or contraband goods — a pleasing but poisonous drug, which, by defeating or destroying the law, would ruin the industry, comfort, happiness, and lives, of all who are benefited by the law. It is, therefore, the duty of the sovereign to see the law respected; but, should his civil agents transcend its prescribed limits, the law, or the monarch, and, least of all, the religion, of the nation and of the Catholic world, should not be censured for it.

If, after an attentive perusal of the following " Letters on the Spanish Inquisition," anti-Catholic prejudice has in any one instance been removed, or the menacing machinations of a set of men who pretend to a Christian character and divine commission, yet systematically abuse the venerable Church of Christ, be to any extent exposed; if the cause of Catholicity, or the rights and liberties of republican America, be in any way benefited by the publication of those letters, — the translator will feel himself sufficiently recompensed for his labors. As to any additional reward, which must depend upon the purity of his intention, and his object, (however willing, yet weak, his efforts are to render a service to his country, his church, and his God,) he humbly hopes he may receive it out of that treasury " where neither the rust nor the moth doth consume, and where thieves do not break through nor steal."

LETTER I.

Sir,

I FELT extreme satisfaction in exciting your interest and astonishment, in the course of my observations on the subject of the Spanish Inquisition. Numerous were the conversations which we have had about this famous institution. As it was your great desire that I should imbody my remarks, and give them a suitable form, I cheerfully comply with your wishes, and accordingly seize this opportunity of laying before you a host of authority which could not be so well brought forward in the course of our colloquial recreations.

Without further preface, therefore, I shall commence the history of this tribunal.

I distinctly remember to have mentioned to you, in general, that the most honorable monument of the Inquisition was the very official report by which this tribunal was suppressed in the year 1812, by the Cortes of *philosophic* memory, whose object, in the evanescent career of their *absolute* power, was self-aggrandizement.* If you reflect upon the feel-

---

* See *Informe sobre el Tribunal de la Inquisicion con el projecto de decreto acerca de los Tribunales protectores de la Religion*, &c. &c., Cadiz, 1812.

ings of that assembly, and particularly of the private committee who drew up the report, you will acknowledge that any declaration favorable to the Inquisition, and emanating from such a source, precludes all reasonable reply. Some modern infidels, the echoes of Protestantism, would fain impose a belief upon the world that Saint Dominick was the author of the Inquisition; and they have, with their usual *consistency*, assailed him with unmeasured declamatory abuse. The *fact*, however, is, that he never exercised an inquisitorial act, and that the Inquisition, which can be traced as far back as the council of Verona, which was held in 1184,* was not intrusted to the Dominicans until 1233; in other words, *twelve years after the death of Saint Dominick.*

The Manichean heresy, better known in modern times by that of the *Albigenses, in the twelfth century, equally threatened the Church and the State.* Ecclesiastical commissioners were deputed to find out the seditious culprits, and were thence called *inquisitors*. Pope Innocent the Third approved of this institution in 1204. The Dominicans first acted as the deputies of the pope and his legates. The Inquisition, so far as they were concerned, was a part of their preaching department, and they were known by the name of *preaching friars*, or *brothers*, which title they still retain. The commencement

---

* Fleury, Eccles. Hist. B. lxxiii. No. liv.

of the Inquisition, like all institutions which are destined to produce great effects, was not what it subsequently became. Called into existence by peculiar circumstances, opinion first sanctions them, and authority, seeing the advantages which are likely to follow, sanctions and gives them a legal form.* Hence it is not easy to specify the precise epoch of the Inquisition, which had a feeble beginning, but which gradually developed its proportionate dimensions, as is the case with whatever is designed to endure. It is, however, an incontestable truth, that the Inquisition, properly so termed, was not lawfully established, with its character and attributes, but by virtue of the bull *Ille Humani Generis* of Pope Gregory IX., addressed to the provincial of Toulouse on the 24th of April, 1233.

It is, moreover, solidly proved *that the first inquisitors, and St. Dominick especially, never opposed heresy with any other arms than those of* PRAYER, PATIENCE, *and* INSTRUCTION. †

You will be pleased to observe here, sir, *en pas-*

---

* As, for instance, the Academies of Science of Paris and London. Those which have been established by edicts are by no means as lawful, and never promise the same success.

† *No opuseron* (los inquisitores) *a los hereges otras armas que la oracion, la paciencia, y la instruccion, entro ellos, S. Domingo como lo asseguran los Bolandos, y los Padres Echard et Touron.* — Vie de S. Dominique, page 20.

See *Encyclop. Methodique*, art. *Dominicains*, and art. *Inquisiteurs*, literally translated by the reporter of the committee, and Feller's *Hist. Dict.*, art. *Dominicains*. It does appear that the *reporter* is mistaken in enrolling St. Dominick in the number of inquisitors. But, even according to his declaration, it is of no consequence.

sant, that we must never confound the character, and, as it were, the primitive genius, of any institution, with the variations which the necessities or passions of men force it to undergo in the course of time. The Inquisition is, in its very nature, good, mild, and preservative. It is the universal, indelible character of every ecclesiastical institution; you see it in Rome, and you can see it wherever the true Church has power. But if the civil power, in adopting this institution, judges it necessary, for its own safety, to render it severe, the Church is not answerable for that severity.

About the fifteenth century, Judaism deeply shot its roots into the soil of Spain, and threatened to kill the national plant.

The riches and influence of the Jews, and their intermarriage with the most distinguished families of the government, rendered them truly formidable. They were, indeed, a nation contained within another.* Mahometanism prodigiously increased the danger; that tree had been pulled down in Spain, but its roots were unimpaired. The great question then was, whether the nation could continue its Spanish character and independence, or whether Judaism and Islamism would divide the spoil of these rich provinces, if superstition, despotism, and barbarity, were to drive their triumphal cars over the

---

* *Por la rigueza e poder que gozaban, y por sus enlaces con las familias mas ilustres y distinguidas de la monarquia era verdudamente un pueblo incluido in otro pueblo*, &c. — Ibid. p. 33.

rights and lives of mankind. The Jews were nearly masters of Spain, and between the high-blooded Castilians and the degenerate sons of Israel no good feeling existed. Their hatred was mutual, and was often carried to excess. The Cortes cried aloud for the adoption of severe measures against the latter. An insurrection broke out in the year 1391, and a dreadful slaughter ensued. The danger daily increased, and Ferdinand, surnamed the Catholic, supposed that, in order to save the country from utter ruin, it was indispensably necessary to establish the Inquisition, as best calculated to cure the political cancer which was rapidly corroding the heart of the nation.

Isabella was at first opposed to the measure, but the arguments and motives of her royal consort finally prevailed, and Pope Sixtus IV., in 1478, despatched the bulls of institution.*— Allow me, sir, before I proceed farther, to present to your consideration a most important remark, viz., *great political evils, and especially violent attacks levelled at the body of a state, can never be prevented or repelled but by measures equally violent.*

It is a political axiom, which no sensible man ever denied.

The rule of ancient Rome is the great standard by which every imaginable danger is to be graduated, viz., " *Videant consules, ne respublica detrimentum*

---

* Ibid. p. 27.

capiat," (*Let the consuls see that the government sustain no injury.*)* As to the *means* of effecting this important end, *by excluding every thing in the shape of crime,* the most successful is invariably the best. If you confine your reflection to the severity of Cardinal Torquemada, and not consider the awful desolation which it prevented, reasoning is useless. Let us, therefore, incessantly bear in mind this fundamental truth, that THE INQUISITION WAS, IN ITS COMMENCEMENT, REQUIRED AND ESTABLISHED BY THE KINGS OF SPAIN, IN PERILOUS AND EXTRAORDINARY CIRCUMSTANCES.† The committee of the Cortes expressly declare it, and that, *circumstances having changed*, the Inquisition became useless. ‡

People were astonished at inquisitors putting repeated questions to an accused individual, in order to *ascertain whether any Jewish or Mahometan blood circulated in his veins*. "*What harm,*" Short-sightedness would say, "*of what use, would it be to know who was the grandfather or great grandfather of the accused?*" But, sir, in *those* days, it was of immense importance to ascertain the fact; because these two proscribed classes of people, having *at*

---

* *This frightful commission immediately vested them with boundless power.*

† *Hallandose in circumstancias tan difíciles y extraordinarias.* Report, p. 37.

‡ *Mas no existindo estas causas, en los tiempos presentes*, &c. (Ibid.) Consequently these causes did exist formerly, and justified the institution.

that time a host of connections in the state, should necessarily either feel or inspire terror.*

It was therefore necessary to make a salutary impression upon the minds of these people, by continually holding forth the anathema which was attached even to the suspicion of Judaism or Mahometanism. It is a great error to suppose that we can get rid of a powerful enemy by merely checking him: prudence tells us that we should drive him at least into his intrenchment.

If we except a very small number of learned men, you will uniformly find, when speaking of the Inquisition, that there are three capital errors riveted, as it were, on the public mind, and which seem to be uninfluenced by the most powerful demonstration.

The three errors are the following: —

1st. *That the Inquisition is a purely ecclesiastical tribunal.* It is false.

2d. *That the ecclesiastics who sit on the tribunal condemn certain culprits to death.* It is false.

3d. *That persons are condemned for the expression of mere opinions.* It is false.

---

* *Porque sus enlaces con familias Judias o Moriscas les hacen suspechosas, habiendo sida instituida principalmente la Inquisicion contra la heregia llamada del Judaismo y del Mahometanismo.* (Ibid. p. 67, I.) I here observed, with due deference to the committee, that the expression, " *the heresy which is called Judaism,*" is ridiculously false.

The Tribunal of the Inquisition is purely Royal.

It is the king who appoints the inquisitor-general; and he, in his turn, nominates the private inquisitors, with the royal consent.

The constitutional charter of this tribunal was published, in 1484, by Cardinal Torquemada, *in concert with the king.**

The inferior inquisitors could do nothing without the approbation of the general; nor could he, without the immediate concurrence of the supreme council. This council *was not* established by the pope's bull; so that, the office of inquisitor-general having become vacant, the members of the council proceed in their individual capacity, *not as ecclesiastical*, but as *royal*, judges. †

The inquisitor, by virtue of the bull of the sovereign pontiff, and the king, by that of his royal prerogative, constitute the authority which regulates, and has constantly directed, the inquisitorial tribunals, — tribunals which are both ecclesiastical and royal; so that, should either of the two powers dissent from the other, the business is necessarily suspended. ‡

---

* *De amerdo con el rey.* — Ibid. p. 32.

† Ibid. pp. 34, 35.

‡ *El inquisitor, en virtud de las bulas de S. S. y el rey en razon de las que le competen por el poder real, constituyen la autoridad que arregla y ha arreglado los Tribunales de la Inquisicion; Tribunales, que a un mismo tiempo son ecclesiasticos y reales: qualquer poder de los dos que no concurra interrompe necessariamente el curso de su expedicion.* — Ibid. p. 36.

The committee were pleased to inform us that these two powers were equally balanced; but you are aware, sir, that no rational man could be duped into such a belief. *The Inquisition is a purely royal instrument; it is entirely in the hands of the king; and any mischief which might result from it must be attributed to the ministry of the crown.* If the proceedings be not regular, if the proofs be not clear, the counsellor of the king, in every capital case, can by a single word quash the suit. The voice of Religion, or of her priests, is never felt or heard on such an occasion.

If the accused were unfortunately punished, though innocent of the charge for which he suffered, the fault and the crime must be imputed to the king, for having framed such a law, or to his civil magistrates, who might have unjustly passed the sentence; and this you will shortly see has been the case.

Remember, sir, that, among the numerous declamations which, in the last century, have been published against the Inquisition, you cannot find a single word concerning *this* distinctive character of the tribunal, which, in justice and in truth, ought to have been made.

The infidel Voltaire, whose favorite object was the annihilation of the altar and the throne, has, in his usual hatred to Christianity, falsified and caricatured its picture.

——————————— Ce sanglant tribunal,
Ce monument affreux du pouvoir monacal,

3 *

Que l'Espagne a reçue, mais qu'elle meme abhorre,
Qui venge les autels, mais qui les deshonore,
Qui tout couvert de sang, de flammes entouré,
Egorge les mortels avec un fer sacré.

A hideous set — a bench that reeks with gore —
This dire memento of a monkish clan —
With horror Spain accepts. What murderous plan!
With fire and sword their altars they defend —
Defend! no, they disgrace, they mar, their end.

The tribunal, however, thus described, is to be found in a nation remarkable for its wisdom and elevated character: it is (we repeat it) a purely *royal* institution, in which all that is wise and distinguished in the ecclesiastical body may be seen. They take cognizance of real crimes, by virtue of preëxisting and public laws; they pass sentence upon them with a degree of wisdom which is perhaps *unique*, but *they never pronounce death upon the culprit*.

What name, then, in the whole vocabulary of infamy is best adapted to that shameless profligate who would thus portray such a body of men! The demoralizing author of *Joan of Arc* had reason to detest an authority which he well knew would have prevented such an unmixed villain from ruining Spain, had he been born in it. Such criminal absurdities excite the contemptuous sneers of the well-informed; but the untutored vulgar, who never think or judge for themselves, are readily entrapped, and unfortunately duped, by such lying calumnies. Their imaginations are easily wrought upon to view the

Inquisition as a club of stupid and ferocious monks, who, for mere amusement, put men upon the rack, or broil them upon gridirons! Error will occasionally insinuate itself into the minds of sensible persons, and into works which are generally dedicated to the defence of sound principles; hence, in a periodical we have, not long since, read the following strange passage:—

"It is true, whatever may be said to the contrary, that the inquisitors have, until 1783, persevered in a habit rather severe, of solemnly burning persons who did not believe in a God: this was their *tic;* but, if we except this, they were men made up of excellent materials."

The author of such an unfounded assertion has certainly never reflected upon what he thus wrote. What tribunal is there in the universe which, one time or other, had not condemned persons to death? What crime does the civil tribunal commit, which consigns a culprit to the scaffold by virtue of a state law, which enacts such a penalty for an offence of which the accused is found guilty? Where is the Spanish law in which it is asserted that Deism is punishable with death? It would be difficult to contrive a greater absurdity, and it would seem equally impracticable to make even unguarded credulity swallow such nonsense.

Amidst the innumerable errors which the eighteenth century has produced and planted in the human mind, with deplorable success, none has ever astonished and disgusted me more than that which supposes, maintains, and impresses upon the illiterate multitude, that *priests* could condemn a human being to death!! A man is excusable for his ignorance of the religion of *Fo*, and of *Bouddah*, and of *Somonocondom ;* * but what justification can a European plead for his unacquaintance with *catholic or universal Christianity?* What eye has not beheld its immense lustre, which, for upwards of *eighteen hundred years*, has, like the sun in the firmament, illuminated the world? What ear has, during that period, been deaf to the continued chime, — " A SANGUINE ABHORRET ECCLESIA ?" (THE CHURCH ABHORS BLOODSHED.) Who does not know that Catholic priests are prohibited from practising surgery, lest their anointed hands should draw human blood, even for the purpose of effecting a cure?

Who does not know that, in countries where *perfect obedience* is practised, the priest is dispensed from deposing as a witness in all capital proceedings; and that, in states where this privilege has not been allowed him, he enjoys at least the benefit of the *Protestant act*, whereby *he testifies in pure obedience to justice, and sues only for mercy?* Never did a priest, as a functionary of the law, ascend the scaffold. Whenever he appeared on such a tragic stage, his part was to act the martyr for the cause of truth, or

---

* Even so, whoever would undertake to defame them ought first to be acquainted with them. What is the conduct of *interested*, *mercenary* declaimers against the Church of Christ, in this respect? — *Translator*.

as the happy consoler of condemned humanity. He greaches mercy and clemency, and in no part of the plobe did he ever shed any blood but his own.

The Church, the chaste spouse of the Son of God, who, in imitation of her glorious Bridegroom, well knows how to pour out her blood *for* others, but not to draw that *of* others, entertains, with regard to murder, a peculiar horror, and in a manner fully proportionate to the special light which her God has given her. She views men, not only as men, but as likenesses of the God whom she adores. She feels for each a holy respect, which amounts to veneration, knowing that each has been ransomed at an infinite price, so as to become a temple of the living God. She, therefore, believes that the death of a man, who is killed without the order of God, is not only homicide, but a sacrilege, which deprives her of one of her members; for, whether the individual belongs to the household of her faith or not, she invariably considers him either as one of her children, or as capable of becoming so.

Every one knows that private individuals are not allowed to insist upon the death of a fellow-being; and hence arose the necessity of establishing public functionaries to require it on the part of the king, or government, or rather on the part of God. Therefore it is that the civil powers exercise this right only *according to the deposition of witnesses*, and, as such, act as faithful dispensers of the divine power in depriving men of life; consequently they must conscientiously pronounce sentence, in conformity to the laws, and consign only those to an ignominious and awful fate whom the laws condemn. If, however, the order of Deity obliges them to see that the laws are carried into effect in relation to the bodies of criminals, the same divine order compels them to make a suitable provision for the souls of such unfortunate beings. All this is meritorious and becoming; and, nevertheless, *the Church holds the effusion of blood in such abhorrence that she deems all who abet, promote, and effect, a capital condemnation of a fellow-being, although it be accompanied by every religious consideration, to be disqualified from officiating at her altars.**

Behold, then, sir, a beautiful theory. But you are probably curious to know the actual, the true spirit of the holy priesthood upon this important point. Study it, then, in countries where the Catholic Hierarchy has swayed, and still holds, the sceptre of power. A circle of ecclesiastical sovereignties was, owing to peculiar, to extraordinary circumstances, established in Germany; and, to judge of the effect of the justice and popular benefit which they produced in the social compact, it may be sufficient to remind you of the old German proverb, — "*Un term Krummstabe ist gut wohnen;*" in other words, *It is good to live under the crosier.*

---

* Pascal, XIVth Provincial Letter. — Infamous as this writer was, he, notwithstanding, sometimes told the truth. Erat quod tollere velles.

Proverbs, which are the voice of facts and result of popular experience, are never known to mislead. To such a testimony, therefore, do I appeal, and it is gratifying to reflect that it is further corroborated by the unanimous suffrage of all who have any pretension to judgment or recollection. Never was there any question proposed, in these mild and pacific governments, of any persecution or capital conviction of the spiritual enemies of the reigning powers.

But what shall we say of Rome? It is unquestionably here, in the government of the sovereign pontiff, that the genuine spirit of the priesthood ought to be unequivocally displayed.

Now, sir, it is a universally-admitted fact, that this government was never upbraided *but for its mildness*. In no spot of the civilized world can there be found a government more paternal, justice more impartially administered, a system of restraint which is at once more humane and judicious, and a toleration more instructively perfect.

Rome is probably the only part of Europe where the Jew feels himself neither maltreated nor humbled. Yes, Rome is the holy, the liberal, the charitable, the enlightened spot, where he feels most happy, and which the persecuted Israelite has, almost from time immemorial, distinguished by the glorious title of "*the Jewish paradise.*"

Open the page of history, and then answer, what sovereignty has ever exhibited more clemency to anti-religious crimes of every description? Such was the uniform tenor of Christian, Catholic Rome, even at the epoch which has been termed the dark ages of ignorance and fanaticism. Allow me, sir, to remind you of the conduct of POPE CLEMENT THE FOURTH, who, in his letter to Louis, king of France, *rebuked* him for the severity of the laws which that monarch enacted against blasphemers.* The supreme pontiff, the vicegerent of the Prince of mercy, requested him, in the official declaration bearing date July 12, 1268, to mitigate forthwith their asperity, and observed to the king of Navarre, in a bull of the same date, that "*It is by no means proper to imitate our dear son in Jesus Christ, the French king, in relation to the extremely rigorous laws which he has enacted against crimes of this sort.*† Voltaire, when his anti-religious fever had not obtained an ascendency over his justice and judgment, paid a most honorable tribute to the papal government. I shall quote it. You can find the remarkable passage in his poem on the *Natural Law*.

Marc-Aurele et Trajan melaient au champ de Mars
Le bonnet du pontife au bandeau des Cesars.

---

* See the notes of Du Cange on Joinville. Collection des Memoires concernant l'Histoire de France, tome ii. p. 258, note 3.

St. Louis ordered that the tongues of blasphemers should be perforated, if I mistake not, with a red-hot iron. This was an awful punishment. It is worthy of notice, however, that blasphemy, when clearly established, is death by the law in some modern and well-governed nations.

† Sed fatemur quod in pœnis hujusmodi tam acerbis — charissimum in Christo filium nostrum regem Francorum illustrem non deceat imitari. — Ibid. p. 259.

L'univers reposant sous leurs heureux genie,
Des guerres de l'ecole ignorait la manie,
Ces grands legislateurs, d'un saint zele animes,
Ne combatirent point pour leurs poulets sacres.

Aurelius and Trajan, in Mars' wide field,
(To whose enlightened minds the world did yield
When war scholastic wore no maniac frown,)
Had joined the mitre to great Cæsar's crown.
These noble statesmen, full of zeal and peace,
Fought not for dogmas, nor for *sacred geese.*

Rome encore aujourd'hui, conservant ces maximes
Joint le trone a l'autel par des nœuds legitimès,
Ses citoyens en paix, sagement gouvernes,
Ne sont plus conquerans et sont plus fortunès.

Such maxims even now great Rome upholds,
Joins throne and altar in her lawful folds;
Her happy sons inhale the air of peace;
Forgetting war, they reap a just increase.*

---

* See his poem on *Natural Religion*, IVth part. It is, indeed, singular that Voltaire, who may be called inconsistency personified, who is reasonable and just in what he here says of the government of modern Rome, should lose sight of reason in the immediately preceding verses. How, it may be asked, and with whom, were the Romans to fight for their *sacred geese?* Did any nation advance in arms to seize or slaughter these *geese?* If any new god were presented to pagan Rome, he was introduced by the permission of the senate, as a newly-canonized saint (pious minds will, I hope, pardon the comparison) is brought into our Church. Such a process may not come under the signification of the term *toleration;* but however slight is the allusion to the basis of natural religion, Voltaire might have seen in the history of the Bacchantes, which is well described by Livy, (xxxix. 9, sqq.,) how they would have been treated. When Christianity appeared, *these great legislators* began to persecute it with unparalleled ferocity. It has been remarked that the monstrous Tiberius, Caligula, Commodus, &c. &c., did not molest the new religion; while the *philosophers*, Trajan, Antoninus, Marcus Aurelius, and Julian, were its uncompromising enemies. (*Feller's Hist. Dict.*, art. *Marcus Aurelius.*) — It is, therefore, incon-

Now, sir, allow me to ask you, How can such a glorious character, stamped with a seal of unclouded evidence, be positively falsified in a comparatively small corner of the globe? By what kind of magic or *legerdemain* does it happen that a religion essentially mild, tolerant, charitable, and consolatory, throughout every nation of the earth, should wear, in Spain, (which is proverbially noble and generous,) the horrid costume of bloody extermination?

This is a question of the greatest importance; and, in the examination of every subject which comes within the range of human consideration, there is nothing so essential as to avoid a confusion of ideas. When, therefore, we speak of the Inquisition, let us fairly separate and clearly distinguish the civil from the ecclesiastical power.

Whatever severity, terror, or death, the Inquisition inflicts, is exclusively caused and performed by the government. It, and it alone, is responsible for every act of this tribunal. Clemency, which, like the tutelary angel, performs so conspicuous a part in all its proceedings, is the uniform feature of the Church, who never interferes, except it be to arrest or mitigate the tortures of the culprit.

---

testably certain that the sovereign Christian pontiffs never did persecute; whereas the infidel Voltaire was guilty of a malicious and an unpardonable falsehood, when he compared them to the pagan emperors and heathen pontiffs, Marcus Aurelius and Trajan. The insipid panegyrists of *toleration* in pagan Rome should have recollected at least one passage of the above-cited historian, viz., *The Ediles are charged to see that no god shall be admitted in Rome, if he be not a Roman, and adored after the Roman custom.*—iv. 30.

Such is the indelible, immutable character of the Church of Christ; and it is not only an error, but even a crime, to suppose, much more to maintain, that Catholic priests can be in any way instrumental in compassing the death of a fellow-being.

In the history of France, there is a prominent fact, which, notwithstanding, has not been sufficiently noticed: I allude to the KNIGHTS TEMPLARS. These noble-minded, but unfortunate men, whether criminal or otherwise it is not our present object to inquire, (although the villany of Philip the Fair, and of his rapacious, unprincipled associates, it would seem, leaves no room for doubt on this subject,) earnestly requested to be tried by the tribunal of the Inquisition; "*for they were convinced*," say the historians, "*if they had such judges, that they could not be condemned to death!*" But the king of France, who had *prejudged* them, and who knew the inevitable result of such a reference, convened his state council, and, after *a private audience*, immediately ordered the poor Templars to be *murdered!!!* The reader should not confound these illustrious men with the *mock* Templars, who hail under the *masonic* flag.

According to the very principles of the Inquisition, and at a period which loudly called for the greatest severity, this tribunal confined itself to the confiscation of the criminal's property; and even that sentence was reversed, according to AN ACT OF GRACE, by the criminal abjuring his errors.* According to the

---

* Vide Report, p. 33.

report to which we refer, it is impossible precisely to ascertain at what epoch the inquisitorial tribunal first pronounced a capital condemnation. It is fully sufficient for our purpose, however, to be convinced of an incontestable fact, that it never could have acquired this right, until it became exclusively a royal or political institution; and that every judgment which affects life in any degree was, is, *and must ever be*, most conscientiously discountenanced by the Church. In our days, uncertainty on this point is unknown. We know that in every important sentence, even in case of a simple arrest, nothing is attempted in Spain without the permission of the supreme council; which fact presupposes the greatest prudence and circumspection.* If the accused be declared a *heretic*, the tribunal, after having pronounced sentence of confiscation, hands him over for *legal* punishment to the *secular* power, the council of Castile, the very name of which bespeaks the most wise, erudite, and impartial body of men in the universe.

If the proofs are not irresistible, if the culprits are not obstinately attached to doctrines which, from the lamentable experience of other nations, tend to the subversion of morality, pure religion, and society, they are merely required to abjure them in the Church, according to the prescribed ceremonial.

A certain family stain, and a civil disqualification,

---

* *De entitad.*— Ibid. p. 64.

whereby he can hold no office under the government, are the result; but I am thoroughly convinced that these provisions are clemency in disguise, to save the lives of the greatest criminals. Certain facts, which have come to my knowledge, and especially the character of that tribunal, leave no possible room in my mind to doubt the correctness of such an assertion.

The tribunal of the Inquisition is composed of a supreme chief, who is called the *grand inquisitor*, and is always either an archbishop or bishop, and of eight ecclesiastical counsellors, (six of whom are always seculars, two are regulars,) one of whom must be of the Dominican order, by virtue of a privilege which was granted by King Philip III. The second, by rotation of office, belongs to the other regular orders, according to a provision made by King Charles III.

To the youngest member of this ecclesiastical council are intrusted the fiscal concerns.

There are certain cases, of which I have not a perfect knowledge, wherein two counsellors from Castile attend. I presume, however, that they are convoked whenever capital punishment is called in question.*

This simple, incontestable description puts to

---

* *La Inquisicion sin mascara, o disertacion en que se prueba hasta la evidencia los vicios de este tribunal y la necessitad de que se suprima. Por Natanael Tomtob.* (This looks like an anagram.) Cadiz. Niel. 1811, in 8vo.

I endeavor to quote only the works which are decidedly hostile to the Inquisition, in order to avoid every mistake in whatever they contain in any manner favorable to this tribunal.

flight the malicious phantoms of the impious Voltaire, of his slanderous associates, and of his ignorant, yet vituperative imitators. What influence can two counsellors of a regular order have upon a body consisting of eleven or thirteen? As to those poor and calumniated Dominicans on whom our prejudice has so long and ungenerously fastened all the odium to which the Inquisition has mysteriously given rise, justice and honor oblige us to confess the cruel injury offered to their reputation, and, by such an avowal, to express our sorrow for the offence, and to become henceforward more cautious and charitable.

Were we to reflect upon the constituent members of this tribunal, it would, indeed, be difficult to conceive one better calculated to remove every possible suspicion of cruelty, and, I am justified in saying, every shadow of severity. Whoever is acquainted with the spirit of the Catholic priesthood must be convinced, on cool and dispassionate examination, that mercy necessarily sways the sceptre of that tribunal. Another circumstance, which deserves particular notice, is the fact that, independently of the favorable presumption which grows out of such an inquisitorial body, it, moreover, presupposes an infinite degree of mildness, which experience clearly proves, and which is invariably thrown into the scale of the accused. Without dwelling further upon this point, I shall now lay before you a sentence of the Inquisition of the most severe kind — a sentence which, without *ordering*, (and this is a possible case,) yet *prepares the way for death,* when cognizance is taken of a crime which the law of the state visits with the loss of life.

"We have declared, and do hereby declare, the accused, N. N., to be convicted as an heretical apostate,* a favorer and abettor of heretics, a false and counterfeit penitent,† and an impenitent relapser; by which crimes he has incurred the penalty of high excommunication, and the confiscation of all his property to the benefit of the royal chamber and the treasury of his majesty.‡ We declare, moreover, that said accused, N. N., ought to be, and he hereby is, abandoned to justice and the secular arm. *We, however, beg and most affectionately charge, in the strongest and best manner in our power, that he may be treated with kindness and mercy.*"

The Spanish author of "*The Inquisition Unmasked,*" from which production I take these details, really pretends that this clause of "kindness and mercy" is a mere formality, which produces no real

---

* The question, then, is not concerning a *pure*, or *mere* heretic, but a heretical apostate; that is, a *Spanish* subject convicted of having apostatized, and given external proofs of it; *otherwise no suit would have been instituted.*

† The declaration is levelled against the *relapser*. The culprit who acknowledges his crime, and says, "*I have sinned, and am truly sorry for it,*" is invariably pardoned. Such mercy is unparalleled in the records of any other bench in the universe. If, notwithstanding, he returns, like the dog to its vomit, to the same errors, after having received pardon, he is declared a *false and counterfeit penitent.*

‡ Thus the tribunal is purely *royal*, in spite of the *ecclesiastical fiction;* and all the unmeaning verbiage about *sacerdotal avarice,* &c. &c. &c., may well be considered as "trifles light as air."

benefit. He cites Van-Espen, according to whom this protestation, as entered by the tribunal, is a sort of external form, *which is, however, dear to the Church.*

This objection does not in the least affect our original position, viz., *that the Inquisition never condemns to death, and that the name of a Catholic priest is never to be found in the document of a capital conviction.**

When the Spanish law punishes certain crimes with death, secular justice cannot contravene that law; and if the Inquisition, as is always the case, never condemns except upon the strongest evidence, the decrees of that body in capital cases will be surely followed by death, while this tribunal does not, in the slightest degree, participate in it; so that the following assertion is uniformly true, viz., "The condemnation does not take place until the secular authority is at perfect liberty to act according to its understanding;" so that, if, by virtue of the specified clause, "so dear to the Church," the royal judges punished innocence, they would be the first who were guilty.

---

* It may not be uninteresting to present the reader with the very words of the declaration, in the Spanish language: —

"Declaramos al dicho N. N. haber sido y ser herege apostata, fautor y encubridor de hereges (quando es relapso) ficto y simulado confitente, impenitente relapso, y por ello haber caido y incurrido en sentencia de excommunication mayor . . . . y en confiscation y perdimiento de todos sus bienes, los quales mandamos applicar y applicamos alla camara y fisco real de S. M. . . . . y que debemos de relaxar y relaxamos la persona del dicho N. N. a la justicia y brazo secular . . . . a los quales [the secular judges] rogamos y encargamos muy affectuosamente como de derecho mejor podemos, se hayan benigna y piedosamente con el." (Ibid. p 180, 181.) Van-Espen, Jus Ecclesiast. Univ. part ii. tit. x. cap. iv. No. 22.

Thus the expression "*bloody tribunal,*" &c., has, in the present instance, no real meaning.

There is not, there cannot be, a tribunal upon earth which must not feel uncomfortable and unhappy in condemning a fellow-creature to death, yet which can, or ought to be reproached for so doing, when it becomes its solemn and necessary duty to execute the law upon the most positive and unequivocal facts, especially when it would be criminal in it to act otherwise.*

Besides, the tribunal of the Inquisition does not condemn to death the violator of the law. This belongs to the *purely civil* authority, notwithstanding certain appearances to the contrary. What will the anti-inquisitors say now? The remarks of the committee of the Cortes are here in perfect unison with those of the author of the "INQUISITION UNMASKED," to which we have just alluded. "Philip II.," says he, "the most absurd of princes, was the real founder of the Inquisition. His refined policy raised him to

---

* It may not be amiss to notice a favorite phrase of the numerous writers who have been decidedly hostile to the Inquisition, and how the expression has originated. All culprits who are condemned by this tribunal are called *victims of the Inquisition!*

They *are* victims only inasmuch as are all *criminals* who are found guilty, and punished by every judicial power throughout the world. It should be remembered that the Inquisition transfers the accused to the secular department for trial, in cases of extreme necessity and importance; for nothing is so true and obvious to all who *will* understand, as the remark of an anonymous Italian writer, who wrote on this subject about twenty-eight years ago. His words run thus: "*Il tribunale del S. Officio non abandonna* [a correct expression] all' ultimo supplicio che gente di perduta coscienza e rei delle piu oribili empieta. (Della punizion degli Eretici, e del tribunale della S. Inquisizione. Roma, 1795, in 4to. p. 133.)

this high degree of pride. Kings have always rejected the counsels and suspicions which had been presented to them against this tribunal, *because they are in all cases absolute masters of nominating, suspending, or revoking, the inquisitors, and have, moreover, nothing to apprehend from the Inquisition, which is terrible only to the subjects."* *

I avail myself of this formal declaration of the committee, for the purpose of showing that the priesthood should not be maliciously implicated; and, if further proof were necessary, you may find it in the report itself, where the reporter of said committee observes that in none of the pope's bulls can it be ascertained that the business of the supreme council can be transacted in absence of the inquisitor-general, which inconvenience, however, is easily remedied, inasmuch as (and he concludes very correctly) *the counsellors act in this case not as ecclesiastical, but royal, judges.*† Do we not know that it is a settled point, that, at the present day, as formerly, no ordinance of the Inquisition can be executed, nor even published, without the previous consent of the king? ‡

Hence it happens that the kings have always tenaciously adhered to this civil institution, and that

---

* Porque son (los Reyes) en todo caso, los arbitros de suspender nombrar y revocar a los Inquisitores, &c. — p. 68.

† Page 35.

‡ *Hoy mismos .... los edictos de la Inquisicion no podian publicarse sin haber antes obtenido el consentimiento del rey.* — p. 80.

Charles V. among others, having been solicited by the states of Arragon and Castile to mitigate its severity, returned, in his usual policy, a very ambiguous answer, which had the *appearance* of his compliance, but which, in fact, was otherwise.* The historian, therefore, whose assertion on such an occasion is by no means to be suspected, was perfectly fair, when he declared that *the religious Inquisition was, to all intents and purposes, a political Inquisition.*†

It is very remarkable that, in the year 1519, the people of Arragon had obtained from Pope Leo X. the object of their petition; and this fact would show the universal spirit of the Church, as well as the character of the sovereign pontiffs. Charles V., however, opposed the operation of these bulls, and the pope, who did not wish to offend this monarch, issued another in 1520, whereby he approved of Charles's conduct, on *ascertaining that the audacious and revolutionizing character of the impious Lutheran doctrine, which menaced all the civil and religious institutions of Germany, imperiously required it.*‡

Now, sir, permit the reporter to declare that the establishment of the Inquisition is absolutely null, because it had not the approbation of the Cortes, and especially *that this tribunal is incompatible with the sovereignty of the nation.*§

---

* Ibid. p. 50.
† Garnier, Hist. de Charlemagne, tome ii chap. iii. p. 481.
‡ Ibid. p. 52.   § Ibid. p. 65.

As for my part, I am willing to allow the Spaniards to settle the question of the people's sovereignty as they think proper, with their king, *by the grace of God*, Ferdinand VII.: let them be particularly mindful to ask his majesty, with the reporter of the committee, "*How does the nation exercise its sovereignty in the judgments of the Inquisition*"? *Positively in no way.** Such frankness cannot but make a deep impression upon the mind of the monarch. What shall I say of that famous expression, which should be written in letters of gold, wherein the reporter eloquently describes the terrible tribunal *tearing away, at the midnight hour, the husband from the bosom of his affectionate wife*, &c? There is no man, I can assure you, sir, less disposed than I am to excite the alarms of woman, and especially in the night-time; and I further declare, that, in all the works of politics and law which I have read in the course of my life, I do not remember to have met an instance of a culprit who had not been arrested in open day, from an apprehension of intimidating the wife of the prisoner, and in order that justice, previous to the arrest, may have been conscientiously informed whether the individual was married or single, dissipated or industrious. How flimsy and contemptible, therefore, must the rhetoric of brainless and malicious declaimers appear, when contrasted

---

* *¿De que modo exerce la Nacion la soberania en los juicios de la Inquisicion? — De Ninguno*, p. 66. The reporter is here certainly right; he only forgets (and the omission is no doubt unintentional) that this reproach is intended for all the tribunals.

with solid reality! After having furnished you with a few specimens of such revolutionary characters, allow me to lay before you an extract from the Madrid Gazette:—*

"It pleased our lord, the king, (whom God preserve,) to honor with his august presence, on the 14th April last, about nine o'clock, A. M., the holy office hotel of the *Court* Inquisition. His majesty visited all the rooms, and even the prisons, and took pains to be most minutely informed of all, and to render the most satisfactory justice to the manifest zeal with which the ministers of this tribunal serve the two MAJESTIES.† During this visit, which lasted nearly three hours, the king was constantly accompanied by his excellency, the inquisitor-general, who was complimented in having waited upon his majesty, and given him satisfactory answers." ‡

This superior magistrate thus addressed his royal master at the moment of departure:—

"*Sire,*

"*God, who, by His just and incomprehensible judgments, thought proper that the tribunal of the*

---

* El tribunal del Santo Officio de la Inquisicion de Cortes. — *Gazetta de Madrid*, April, 1815. This passage proves that all is referred to the royal power.

† *En obsequio de ambas magestades.* How correct an expression! how sensible! how true! The monarchy, unity, independence, of each, and yet a perfect union. Thus the great Bossuet thought when he made use of the words *the two sovereignties.*

‡ This title, and the distinctive appellation of the three inquisitors subsequently mentioned in the same page, prove that none of them belonged to a religious order.

faith should drink to the very dregs the cup of bitterness, has rescued your majesty from captivity, and reëstablished you upon the throne of your ancestors, to become the restorer, consoler, and protector of the Inquisition.

"*Your majesty, after having visited the supreme council, condescends to honor with his presence the court tribunal, and to examine all its dependencies. Permit me to ask you, sire, has your majesty seen* those subterraneous prisons, those frightful dungeons, those instruments of torture, *about which the enemies of the throne and the altar have talked so much in their crazy moments? Have you seen the ministers of the God of peace changed into so many Neros and Diocletians, lighting up the pile, and indulging in all the cruelty which the most systematic barbarity could devise?*

"*Your majesty has seen that the prisons are decent, even comfortable, and that the ministers of the holy office know how to temper justice with mildness and mercy. God grant that the visit of your majesty may be the means of rectifying the errors of such men as have abandoned the way of truth! The court tribunal, affected with the most lively gratitude, shall never cease to supplicate the Father of light that He may vouchsafe to grant your majesty discernment and wisdom for the adoption of such measures as are best suited to such critical circumstances, and the happiness of* REIGNING ALONE*

---

* These two words have a forcible signification.

over your Catholic subjects, who are worthy of the Spanish name."

I doubt whether a president of the STAR CHAMBER ever addressed *his* royal master in similar language. Such a tone, and all the other proofs, however, are necessary merely for those who have not sufficiently reflected upon the nature of things, which not only dispense with, but even anticipate, every thing in the shape of proof.

The character of the Inquisition cannot be too strongly and frequently described, on account of the numberless calumnies with which it has been assailed by individuals who were *perfectly ignorant of it;* and if you choose to know, sir, how prejudice and party spirit can influence men who are otherwise sensible and well informed, you have only to read the following new charge of the committee :—

"Philip II.," say they, "prohibits an appeal, as he considers it an abuse of the decisions of this court; so that it is independent of all civil authority,* and the grand inquisitor is a sovereign in the midst of a sovereign nation, or inasmuch as he is placed on the right hand of a sovereign. He condemns Spanish subjects according to the civil law, without any secular interference or influence." † They inform us, immediately after, that "the Inquisition is a royal authority; that the inquisitor is a royal agent; and

---
* Page 61. † Page 66.

that all his ordinances are null and void, unless they have the royal sanction; that the royal power nominates, suspends, and revokes at will, every member of this selfsame tribunal; and that, the very moment royal authority would disappear, this tribunal would accompany it." What, then, sir, shall we now say of this *worthy gentleman*, Philip II., who is *a little versed* in the science of governing, and who, *to act conscientiously*, keeps *a second sovereign* at his side? You are, methinks, tempted to exclaim, that sensible men must be shocked at such stories! Alas! no, sir; such men have only to take their seats as members of a deliberative body, and during the agitation of a question which involves principle, party, prejudice, and passion. Let us, therefore, henceforward feel disposed to pardon such aberrations, and yet guard against their seductive tendency. Indulgence is never lawful when it becomes an abettor of falsehood, or a promoter of mischief.

I have the honor to be, sir, &c.

Moscow, June 13, 1815.

LETTER II.

Sir,

Upon the absurd supposition that the Inquisition is a purely ecclesiastical tribunal, and that *Catholic priests* can condemn a man to death, it requires nothing more to complete the infamous picture of malevolent ignorance than to fancy that this tribunal condemned individuals to death for mere opinions, and that a Jew was burnt alive for no other crime than that of his being a Jew!! Such an impious, anti-Catholic calumny had been so often repeated, that it finally was believed to be true. I am sorry to find in the ranks of such inexcusable calumniators Montesquieu himself, who, with unparalleled hardihood in the pretended remonstrance of an *imaginary* Jewess, swelled the tale into a chapter, in his "Spirit of Laws."* To burn an innocent young girl in the metropolis of a European city, merely for her conscientious belief in the religion which she professed, would be a crime of such magnitude and national degradation, as to condemn not only the people or country where the horrid

---

* Livre xxv. chap. xiii.

crime was perpetrated, but the very age in which it occurred. Happily for the honor of the civilized world, the calumny *wore the mark of the beast*, and was stamped with its own damnation, while it buries in infamy the unprincipled author of such a falsehood. How long will beings, who call themselves men, take the unholy liberty of vilifying nations? How long will they be permitted to insult the legally-established authorities of those nations, and to attribute to them acts of the most atrocious tyranny, not only without adducing a solitary fact to substantiate their infamous assertions, but even in direct opposition to unquestionable facts?*

In Spain and Portugal, as elsewhere, persons are unmolested as long as they conduct themselves in a peaceable and becoming manner. An imprudent man, however, whether a dogmatizing knave, fanatic, or fool, who disturbs the smooth current of social life and public order, has to blame himself for any salutary measures which a wise government may adopt for the preservation of general safety and happiness. In the whole range of the civilized world, you will not find, I shall not say a Christian or Catholic, but even a wisely-regulated, nation,

---

* There is a remarkable trait in that unwarrantable chapter, viz., the declaration which the power of truth forces him, though unconsciously, to make, through the Jewess: "*Will you allow us frankly to express your feelings? You consider us rather as your own enemies, than as the enemies of your religion.*" (Ibid. livre xxv. chap. 13.) "There's the rub." Away, then, with the implication of religion; and impute — as is the fact — every capital punishment to the *civil* authority.

which has not thundered forth its capital punishments against those who attempt to subvert its established religion. What signifies the mere name of the tribunal which inflicts such a penalty on the culprits? Such characters are every where punished as they ought to be.* No man has a right to interrogate the kings of Spain, why they thought proper to enact certain punishments for certain crimes. They, as it is natural to suppose, are best acquainted with their own affairs. They know their enemies, and treat them as they judge proper. The great, the only, and incontestable point is, that, for the crimes to which I allude, no man is punished unless by virtue of such a universal and acknowledged law, consistently with invariable forms, and by legally-constituted judges, whom the king empowers, and who cannot act contrary to his wishes. This being the real matter of fact, idle, and, what is still worse, slanderous, declamation immediately falls into contempt, and none have a right to complain. Man feels a natural abhorrence at the idea of being tried by his fellow-man; for he knows what man is, and of what he is capable, when passion blinds and hurries him into action. But every one is bound to

---

* It was never suspected, in Europe, that China had established an inquisitorial tribunal, to maintain the purity of her doctrine, the creed and morality of the empire! Its date, however, is very ancient, and the institution extremely severe. It has shed more blood than all the European Inquisitions put together. There are many who cite China as an instance of toleration, but who could not have long lived in it, had they not observed a profound silence. — *Memoires sur les Chinois,* in 4to. i. page 476, note xxvii.

submit tranquilly to the law; for human nature cannot appear in a more imposing and attractive form than when it is displayed by the general, enlightened, disinterested will of the *legislator*, which is substituted for the private, ignorant, and prejudiced will of *man*.

If, therefore, the Spanish law, which is acknowledged by every Spanish citizen, inflicts the penalty of exile, imprisonment, or death, upon every declared and public enemy of a Spanish dogma, what right has any individual to attempt the justification of a criminal who has fully deserved such punishment? With what justice could the culprit himself complain, when he well knew how easily he might have avoided it, namely, by prudently concealing his sentiments?

With regard to the Jews in particular, every scholar must know that the Inquisition prosecuted only the Christian who became a Jew, or the Jewish relapser, (i. e., the Jew who returned to Judaism after having solemnly adopted the Christian religion,) and the preacher of Judaism. The Christian, or converted Jew, who wished to Judaize, was at perfect liberty to leave the country; but if he continued in Spain, he was aware to what danger he was exposed, as was the Jew who had endeavored to proselytize a Christian. No individual can justly complain of a law which is enacted for all.

Considerable noise has been made in Europe concerning the rack of the Inquisition, and the fiery ordeal with which crimes against religion have been punished. The infidels of France wasted much of their crocodile sympathy and philosophic pathos on the occasion; but their flimsy assertions are not proof against the powerful artillery of logic and facts.

The civil inquisitors resorted to the rack, in compliance with the national laws, and because it was adopted by all the Spanish tribunals. The Grecian and Roman laws had sanctioned it. Athens herself, who was universally believed to be *somewhat* acquainted with liberty, subjected even *freemen* to it. All modern nations have employed this terrible means to obtain the truth. I shall not, however, on the *present* occasion inquire whether all those who prattle about the Inquisition exactly understand, or sufficiently reflect upon, what they assert; and whether there were not as strong motives in those times for its employment as there are now for its suppression. However, since the rack is applicable to every other tribunal as well as to the Inquisition, I see no reason why the reproach of the entire should be visited upon the latter. Let the Protestant *Bernard Picart* wear down his etching-needle to the very stump in tracing out his real or imaginary pictures of terror and torture as caused by the judges of the Inquisition; it is useless labor and loss of time. The king of Spain is alone concerned in it. Such daubs, got up by ignorance and malice, may be to him a subject of ridicule or instruction. The

Catholic clergy feel no interest in such things, only so far as philanthropy and mercy are concerned.

Please to observe, sir, that, according to the report of the *court* committee, not only were the inquisitors bound to assist at the punishment, but even the bishop himself was summoned to attend, although he had sent a delegate;* which at once supposes, in this rigorous proceeding, a kind concern and charity which the judges are permitted to exercise. As every important decree, and even that of a simple arrest, cannot be executed without the will of the supreme council,† it is equally certain that the preliminary sentence which prescribed punishment was subjected to the same formality. We must, therefore, grant that the rack of the inquisitorial tribunals was characterized for all the precaution which the nature of things could permit.

Should the king of Spain think it conducive to the solid interests of his nation to abolish the rack, as it has been in England, France, Piedmont, &c., he could do so, as effectually and as consistently as those powers; and the inquisitors would assuredly be the first to applaud him for such a deed; but it constitutes the very climax of folly and injustice to upbraid those men with a practice which modern times allow, and which has been observed in every place, in every age. ‡

---

* Ibid. p. 63. † Ibid. p. 64.

‡ I should have mentioned that, having had an opportunity, in the month of January, 1808, of conversing upon the Inquisition with two

As to the fiery ordeal, it is still, or it has been, a universal custom. There is no necessity for turning over the books of the old Roman laws, which sanctioned and defined this mode of punishment. All nations have resorted to it in cases of great and cry-

---

Spanish noblemen, who travelled for improvement, when I spoke to them of the rack, they looked at each other with an air of surprise, and positively assured me that *they never heard talk of the rack in the proceedings of the Inquisition!* Such a declaration supposes either that this mode of torture was not adopted by the tribunal, or that it was very rarely used.

Relative to the rack, and other kinds of torture that had been so freely and ferociously used in the Tower of London, during the infernal reign of the profligate and licentious Elizabeth, the Protestant she-pope, and supreme head of the English Church, as by act of parliament established, we may be allowed to refer to Note U, at the end of the eighth volume of *Lingard's History of England:* —

"1. The rack was a large, open frame, of oak, raised three feet from the ground. The prisoner was laid under it, on his back, on the floor: his wrists and ankles were attached, by cords, to two rollers at the ends of the frame: these were moved, by levers, in opposite directions, till the body rose to a level with the frame. Questions were then put; and, if the answers did not prove satisfactory, the sufferer was stretched more and more, till the bones started from their sockets.

"2. The scavenger's daughter, so called, was a broad hoop of iron, consisting of two parts, fastened to each other by a hinge. The prisoner was made to kneel on the pavement, and to contract himself into as small a compass as he could. Then the executioner, kneeling on his shoulders, and having introduced the hoop under his legs, compressed the victim close together, till he was able to fasten the extremities over the small of the back. The time allotted to this kind of torture was an hour and a half, during which time it commonly happened that, from excess of compression, the blood started from the nostrils; sometimes, it was believed, from the extremities of the hands and feet. — See *Bartoli*, 250.

"3. Iron gauntlets, which could be contracted by the aid of a screw. They served to compress the wrists, and to suspend the prisoner in the air, from two distant points of a beam. He was placed on three pieces of wood, piled one on the other, which, when his hands had been made fast, were successively withdrawn from under his feet. 'I felt,' says F. Gerard, one of the sufferers, 'the chief pain in my breast, belly, arms, and hands. I thought that all the blood in my body had run into my arms, and began to burst out of my finger ends. This was a mistake; but the arms swelled, till the gauntlets were buried within the flesh. After being thus suspended an hour, I fainted; and, when I came to myself, I found the executioners

ing crimes against the laws which they held most sacred. Throughout Europe, sacrilege, parricide, and high treason, were punished with fire; and as high treason had been defined, in the principles of criminal jurisprudence, to concern and involve two

---

supporting me in their arms: they replaced the pieces of wood under my feet, but, as soon as I was recovered, removed them again. Thus I continued hanging for the space of five hours, during which I fainted eight or nine times.' — *Apud Bartoli*, 418.

"4. A fourth kind of torture was a cell called 'little ease.' It was of so small dimensions, and so constructed, that the prisoner could neither stand, walk, sit, or lie, in it at full length. He was compelled to draw himself up in a squatting posture, and so remained during several days.

"I will add a few lines from Rishton's Diary, that the reader may form some notion of the proceedings in the Tower: —

"'Dec. 5, 1580. Several Catholics were brought from different prisons.

"'Dec. 10. Thomas Cottam and Luke Kirbye, priests, (two of the number,) suffered compression in the scavenger's daughter for more than an hour. Cottam bled profusely from the nose.

"'Dec. 15. Ralph Sherwine and Robert Johnson, priests, were severely tortured on the rack.

"'Dec. 16. Ralph Sherwine was tortured a second time on the rack.

"'Dec. 31. John Hart, after being chained five days to the floor, was led to the rack. Also Henry Orton, a lay gentleman.

"'1581, Jan. 3. Christopher Thompson, an aged priest, was brought to the Tower, and racked the same day.

"'Jan. 14. Nicholas Roscaroc, a lay gentleman, was racked.'

"Thus he continues till June 21, 1585, when he was discharged. See his *Diarium*, at the end of his edition of Sanders."

What diabolical conduct! It far exceeded the cruelty of the monstrous Nero, towards the Catholics of his day. He was a murderous pagan; but that Elizabeth, the head of the Protestant church, and blasphemously termed by the false and sycophantic translators of the English Bible, the "bright occidental star of happy memory," with the Bible before her eyes, and a perfect acquaintance with the Catholic religion, in which she had been brought up, but from which she basely apostatized, and unsparingly persecuted its members, because they were Catholics, and because the notorious illegitimacy of her birth, and her unwarrantable pretensions, prevented the pope from recognizing her as the rightful successor to England's throne, should be guilty of such atrocity in order to *establish* her *thorough godly reformation*, was infernal in the extreme. By their works you will know them. A bad tree cannot produce good fruit. — *Translator*.

powers, *divine and human*, — every crime, at least of a glaring character, which was committed against religion, was considered an act of *treason against Heaven*, and was, therefore, as severely punished as the others. Hence the universal custom of burning heresiarchs and obstinate heretics. In every age, there are certain general notions, or opinions, which influence the actions of its generation, and which are never called in question. It would seem, therefore, that whatever reproach might arise from the adoption of such opinions should be cast upon all, or none, of the individuals of that age. I shall not here expatiate upon the nature of crime and its punishment, nor examine whether capital punishment be useful and just, or whether the degree of torture should be proportioned to the offence, or, finally, how far this terrible right extends. All such questions I consider as foreign to my design. In order, therefore, that the Inquisition should be exempt from censure, it is sufficient for it to pronounce its judicial decisions as other tribunals do, to condemn notorious culprits, to become an organ of the legislative will, and be sanctioned by the sign-manual of the king. A sense of duty obliges me to say that an heresiarch, an obstinate heretic, and a propagator of heresy, should indisputably be ranked among the greatest criminals. The comparative indifference of mankind, in the present times, about religious concerns, has caused thousands to form very erroneous conclusions relative to facts, which, a few centuries ago, were of vital importance to the civilized world. What was then correctly called a holy zeal, heretics have subsequently termed *fanaticism;* which circumstance shows their ignorance of the *real* acceptation of the word, and of the revolution which they endeavored to excite in the empire of language, as they had unfortunately achieved, in by far too large a portion of the moral and religious world. The modern sophist who *vapors* in his study, and writes as he pleases, never takes the trouble of analyzing the horrid tendencies of Luther's arguments. In his ignorance, or malice, he will not trace the THIRTY YEARS' WAR to this desolating source. How different was the conduct, how philosophic and correct were the views, of ancient legislators, who were convinced that those murderous doctrines would be desolating in their effects, and therefore felt themselves justified in suppressing a crime calculated to tear up the foundation of society and bury it in an ocean of blood! The day, however, has arrived when such legislators have no reason to be so much alarmed; yet, when we reflect that the Inquisition would have certainly prevented the French revolution, it is very questionable whether the sovereign, who should entirely put down such a tribunal, would not thereby inflict a deadly wound on the dearest interests of humanity.

The Abbe De Vayrac is, I believe, the first French writer who gave a correct view of the effects of this institution, in his travels through Spain and Italy.*

---

* Amsterdam, 1731, t. i. p. 9.; t. vi. p. 50; t. viii. p. 151, cited in the *Jour. Hist. et Litter.* 1 Feb. 1777, p. 197.

In 1731, he despaired of having his voice heard amidst the astounding din of unrighteous prejudice. "I unhesitatingly declare," says he, "that, if those who are now so clamorous against the Inquisition knew the persons who compose this tribunal, they would use a far different language. . . . . But what is truly deplorable, is the fact that prejudice has so strongly bewildered my countrymen that I utterly despair of their ever conceiving how circumspection, wisdom, justice, and integrity, can be the characteristic virtues of the inquisitors. A man must, indeed, be extremely wicked, or a very great blockhead, to be taken up by this tribunal."

Every sensible person, who has read the preceding remarks, must be forcibly struck with them. If he do but reflect on the character of the constituent judges of this bench, he will immediately conclude that the great tribunals of Spain are matchless in justice, learning, and integrity; and if, with this universal character, that of the Catholic priesthood be associated, conviction, independently of the result of unerring experience, must prove that in no quarter of the globe can there be found more philosophic calmness, circumspection, and humanity, than are united in the tribunal of the Inquisition. Established, as it has been, to operate upon the imagination, and therefore necessarily accompanied by forms both mysterious and severe, to produce the effect which the legislator had in view, the religious principle, notwithstanding, is invariable, is indelible

Amidst the frightful display of the inquisitorial apparatus, it is merciful and mild; and the circumstance of the priesthood of the true Church being in any way concerned with this tribunal renders it *unique.* It wears on its standard a motto necessarily unknown to every tribunal upon earth,— "MISERICORDIA ET JUSTITIA," (*Mercy and justice.*) *Justice* alone characterizes the others,* and mercy belongs only to the sovereign.

Were judges to lean towards mercy, they might be considered rebels, who thus usurp the rights of sovereignty. But when the ecclesiastical power is called in, it requires, as a *sine qua non*, the free exercise of the sovereign prerogative. MERCY accordingly takes *her seat* with JUSTICE, and even is allowed precedence. The accused, who is brought before this tribunal, is at liberty to plead guilty, to sue for pardon, and submit to a religious expiation. The *crime* then bears the character of *sin*, and *punishment* is commuted into *penance*. The culprit prays, fasts, and mortifies his body. Instead of going to the place of execution, he recites the penitential psalms, hears mass, duly examines the state of his conscience, becomes contrite, confesses his sins, and finally is restored to his family and to society. If the crime be enormous, if the culprit obstinately refuse to retract, if he *will* die sooner than to have it

---

* Yet "oft 'tis seen the wicked prize itself buys out the law." So says Shakspeare. He well knew it in his day,— had seen it in *his own* country.— But of this hereafter.— *Translator.*

said that he recanted his errors, or felt sorrow for his transgressions, the *priest* then retires; and when he reappears, it is for the special purpose of consoling the unfortunate victim on his way to the scaffold.

It is rather singular that a distinctive character of the Inquisition has been acknowledged, in the most solemn manner, by a minister of the French republic; and it is curious to see how his work has been reviewed in the Journal from which I extracted a passage in the preceding letter.* We at once perceive that the writer is a man of more sound reflection than the author of said letter.

"Yet," says this worthy journalist, "what tribunal is there throughout all Europe, except the Inquisition, that acquits the culprit when he truly repents and confesses his crime?

"Who is the obstinate individual that affects an irreligious course of conduct, and professes principles which are contrary to those established by law for the preservation of social order, that has not been twice cautioned by the members of this tribunal? If he relapse, if, notwithstanding the warning which he has received, he persist in such conduct, he is arrested; but, should he repent, he is set at liberty. Mr. Bourgoing, whose *religious* opinions could not be suspected when he was drawing this picture of modern Spain, in speaking of the holy office, says,

---

* *Nouveau Voyage en Espagne, par M. Bourgoing. Journal de l'Empire,* 17 *Septembre,* 1805.

'I do publicly avow, in order to pay homage to truth, that the Inquisition might be cited, in our days, as a model of equity.' What a declaration! How would it be treated if we had made it? Mr. Bourgoing, however, has seen in the tribunal only what in reality is an instrument of profound government."

As to the forms, whether severe or terrible, with which the Inquisition has been so frequently reproached, I have been unfortunate enough not to credit them, and should, at least, have been on the spot, to form a correct opinion of them. However that be, if the revolution which has taken place in public sentiment and morals allow any mitigation in this respect, the king is the fountain-head whence it is to come, and the inquisitors, no doubt, would cheerfully coöperate with him.

Perfection is no attribute of man; and where is the institution which is not liable to abuse? Believe me, sir, when I assure you that there is no man less disposed than I am to justify, or even extenuate, needless severity. I shall merely remark that the religious Inquisition of Spain might be well compared to the public Inquisition of Venice, which commanded a useful ascendency over the minds of the people by its mild, dissuasive influence, and which consisted of certain fanciful associations, that were calculated to maintain order, and save much human blood.

So far as Portugal is concerned, it is equally false to suppose that the party accused could, upon slight grounds, have been cast into prison, denied a transcript of the names of the plaintiffs, of the counts, or charges upon which he had been indicted, or that he would have been denied counsel; nay, the prosecutors would not escape punishment if, in the course of trial, it appeared that they were instigated by calumny or malice.*

This tribunal never pronounces sentence of temporal punishment: it only declares the prisoner to be attainted and convicted; and it then devolves upon the secular judges to define the punishment exactly in the manner prescribed and adopted by the Spanish tribunal.

The confiscations go into the royal treasury, and the diocesan bishops have the right to take cognizance of the crime conjointly with the inquisitors.†
I shall, moreover, observe, with regard to the forms, which are more or less severe, that there is not an enlightened power upon earth which, for grand and just objects, has not established, from time to time, certain extraordinary tribunals, almost entirely exempt from the usual forms. I may here cite, as a case in point, the old provostal court in France. The kings of this nation were mad enough to order that the main roads should be perfectly safe! Every

---

* I am quite confident, with regard to Spain, and I cannot doubt that it is otherwise in Portugal, that the counsel of the incarcerated defendant have the freest and most confidential access to him, and that even the judges take great care to ascertain whether said counsel discharge their duty in this respect.

† See *Anecdotes of the Ministry of the Marquis of Pombal.* Warsaw, 1784, in 8vo. B. viii. No. lxxxvii.

traveller accordingly put himself under the special protection of majesty, and any attack or attempt upon his person was considered a species of high treason, which the law punished in the most terrible manner, and with astonishing despatch. Whoever extorted a crown-piece from another was seized by the marshals, delivered up to the great provost, who presided with his two recorders, and was racked to death in twenty-four hours, in presence of the parliament, who in no wise interfered.

Such jurisprudence was not, to be sure, of the most compassionate order; yet it was quite optional in every Frenchman not to rob on the highway, and the king (for even kings have their hobbies) intended that his subjects should not only travel, but even lie down and sleep, if they thought proper, on the highway with perfect safety!

You now perceive, sir, how many accumulated calumnies and errors have been thrown upon the Inquisition by modern would-be philosophers. They have represented it as a purely ecclesiastical tribunal; but I, according to the most unequivocal, unexceptionable authorities, have laid before you its *real* character. Infidel sophisters would fain make the world believe that the Catholic *priests* condemned a man to death! and for a mere opinion, too!

But I have held the mirror up to nature, and shown the subject in its true light; yes, sir, they described the Inquisition as a papal invention, and that the popes granted it only on the solicitation of the sovereigns, and often even so with a manifest degree of repugnance, at least so far as certain privileges were concerned, which to them appeared severe.

To complete the tale, they should have attacked it on the ground of ecclesiastical discipline, by endeavoring to prove, or rather, in their *usual* way, by asserting, that it weakened the jurisdiction of the bishops; but, unfortunately for those "*modern reformers*," the authority of the whole body of the Spanish episcopacy would have overwhelmed them; — a body, at least, as respectable and enlightened as can be found in the universal army of the church militant, and who have expressly declared that they always found in the Inquisition a faithful ally, ever ready to assist in the preservation of the faith. But you know, sir, that party spirit never hesitates and never recoils from its vicious, vituperative course.

The committee of the Cortes have raked out of the neglected rubbish of time a musty anecdote — *we know not of what kind*, whether true or false — of a grand inquisitor — *we know not whom* — who, having prosecuted, in the year 1622 — *we know not how, or why* — a certain bishop of Carthagena — *we know not whom* — was, for this *misdeed*, censured by a consultation, *we know not, of what* council of Castile; and upon this *luminous authority, at once so unequivocal and modern*, the same committee exclaim, with an air of majestic importance, "*After this, how can the right reverend bishops dare, contrary to the testimony of their fellow-brethren, and the authority of* *the first tribunal of the nation*, to represent to your HONORS, (the Cortes,) that they are aided in their episcopal functions in the maintenance of the faith " ? *

A singular *fact*, a *fact* more than doubtful, and by no means minute, a *fact* of the year 1622, opposed to the solemn declaration of the episcopal body, strikes us as one of those prodigies of nonsense which more or less characterize all popular assemblies. With similar *success* do the committee reproach the Inquisition for flinging its shadowy influence over the human mind. *Is it possible*, say they, *that a nation can become illustrious when her mind is buried in such gross slavery! Literature disappeared when the Inquisition was established.*† The committee felt more disposed, on this occasion, to be merry, than correct, witty, or wise. Is there even a sciolist, who does not know that the golden age of literature appeared and bloomed in the reign of Philip II., and that the holy office first stamped their approbation upon the works of those numerous writers, who threw a brilliant halo of intellectual glory around the Spanish name? Yes, mathematics, astronomy, chemistry, medicine, surgery, anatomy, materia medica, natural science, law, philology, his-

---

* *¿ Como pueden pues decir los R. R. Obispos que han representaao a V. M. que los ayudan (los inquisitores) en la conservacion de la fe contra los testimonios de sus cohermanos y autoridad del primer tribunal de la nacion ?* — Ibid. p. 56.

† *¿ Es possible que se ilustre una nacion en la qual se esclavizan tan groseramente los entendimientos ? Ceso de escribirse desdeque se establecio la Inquisicion.* — Ibid. p. 75.

tory, antiquity, &c., are, in all conscience, extensive fields in which the Spanish mind may roam at will, without any let or hinderance from the right reverend fathers of the Inquisition.

Away, then, with the iniquitous assertion, that genius groans in chains, when it is merely prohibited from attacking national dogmas. Error, how often soever repeated, cannot, therefore, command the authority of truth.

I have the honor to be, sir,

Yours, &c. &c.

Moscow, July 2, 1815.

LETTER III.

Sir,

The origin and distinctive characters of the Inquisition which I have laid before you, were exclusively drawn from the committee report of the Cortes, whose object it was to suppress that famous institution. Could I have given a more convincing proof of liberality and unquestionable impartiality? When the defendant substantiates his innocence by the very indictment and witnesses of plaintiff, why should such plaintiff complain? Whom should he blame? Now, sir, to give you correct information of the proceedings of the Inquisition, I shall, in the first place, cite an authority fully as unequivocal as "THE REPORT" itself.

It comes from an *English Protestant*, A PARSON OF THE CHURCH OF ENGLAND! He visited Spain during 1786 and 1787.* It would seem *natural* to suppose, that, when the subject of the Inquisition called his pencil into action, he spared not his *shading* art. He states that, *at a short distance from Seville, there*

---

* *Travels in Spain during the Years* 1786, 1787. By Joseph Townsend, Rector of Pewsey. London, 1792. Second edition, 3 vols. 8vo.

is a building, whose singular form struck him; that, after several questions, which he proposed to a gentleman who accompanied him, he was informed it was called "El Quemadero," while he was requested not to mention the name of his informant.*

He lost no time in retiring from a building which his imagination had surrounded with bloody flames. A man clothed with judicial power told him, on the following day, that this house was reserved for burning heretics, and that, four years ago, a woman had there suffered that cruel death. She had been a member of a religious community, and was guilty of divers infamous acts and plots.

What a tissue of absurdity, from first to last!

Pray, sir, what idea can we form of *a building destined for the burning of heretics?* Would not *itself* be most liable to *suffer* on the very first experiment? *A building for the burning of heretics,* gives us an idea of consummate nonsense. But the best of the *joke* is the request that the English traveller would keep the information as a profound *secret!* A secret relative to a public place destined for capital punishment *by fire!* This is not the only

---

* The place where criminals, condemned to the fire, are burnt. The reader is almost instantaneously reminded of "The Smithfield Fires," near London, where numerous base apostates from the Church of Christ had, for their subsequent *rebellious* and *infamous conduct,* suffered death.

If I be not much mistaken, the term El Quemadero, *in its extensive signification, is applied to the place where this awful sentence is pronounced.*

silly story which heresy has invented for the *instruction* and *edification* of Europe.

I am positive that Spanish gravity was on this occasion ridiculed by Protestant credulity. "*Do you see that building?*" a *Seville* wag might say. "*Heretics are secretly burnt in it; but I beg of you, for the love of mercy, to say nothing about it, for you would thereby ruin me!*"

What is still more amusing, the *reverend* bookmaker speaks of this "QUEMADERO" as if it were a coffee-*roaster*, which is in daily use. *His imagination presented it to him as surrounded with bloody flames.* An inexperienced man would suppose, from such a statement, that our *veracious* traveller had seen a slaughter-house erected in the centre of a permanent bonfire; and yet, strange to add, there had been but one execution in the course of four years! But who was the victim? *A woman who had been a member of a religious community, but who was guilty of divers infamous acts and plots.*

Does not, at least should not, the hand of justice severely punish such culprits in *every* country? The good *clergyman* did not, of course, deem it expedient to enter into a minute detail of the case. His expressions, like his creed, are of the latitudinarian order, and it is laughable to find him at first affirming that *this place was reserved for burning heretics*, and in the same breath mentioning, by way of *proof*, the execution, not of a heretic, but of a monster! In some European countries, which are characterized for their wise government, and the faithful execution of the laws, an incendiary, who sets fire to a house in which a family resides, is *burnt alive*, and every honest citizen exclaims, "*He deserved it.*"

Do you suppose, sir, that a man, who is guilty of immense theoretical and practical infamy, such as your imagination may conceive, is less criminal than such an incendiary? I cannot see why the name of the latter punishment, which has been given to a place of execution, excites a stronger terror in the mind than the ordinary name of said place; nor why, for instance, it would have disgraced France, had she called her *Place de Greve* * the *Rouerie*, or, in other words, "the guillotine-ground" "the racking-place."

Let us now hear the story of a *frightful* auto da fe which had taken place some time before.

A beggar, named *Ignatius Rodriguez*, was tried by the Inquisition for having distributed certain *love-draughts, which consisted of ingredients that modesty would blush to mention.*

Whenever he administered this *ridiculous* medicine,† he pronounced some words of the *black art*

---

* A public place in Paris where criminals suffer death.

† "Ridiculous!" It appears that the English preacher does not view this matter in the light of an austere moralist.

jargon.* It was clearly proved that this philter had been administered to persons of every rank. *Rodriguez* had two accomplices, *Juliana Lopez* and *Angela Barrios*, who were arraigned with him. One of these petitioned for her life, and was informed that *the usage of the holy office was not to condemn to death.*† *Rodriguez* was condemned to ride on an ass through the streets of Madrid, and to be whipped. They further imposed some religious penalty upon him, and he was exiled from the city for five years. The reading of the sentence was frequently interrupted by loud bursts of laughter, in which the beggar himself had freely joined. The culprit was, in fact, paraded through the streets, but not whipped : ‡ he was presented with wine and biscuit by way of refreshment on his journey." § What

---

* We here perceive two distinct crimes narrated with an air of gravity. One is a little more than *ridiculous;* the other is *necromancy;* but it appears, from the statement of the *Protestant divine,* that the Inquisition, with all its cruelty, took no cognizance of it !
I strongly doubt whether, in any other part of the world, a person, when guilty of it, would come off on such easy terms. *What was the* conduct of the *pious Calvinistic Orthodoxy* in Salem, Massachusetts, and in other parts of the world, some years ago, *relative to the burning of witches,* &c. ? *Perhaps more of this anon.* — *Translator.*

† Yet this tribunal, as we have already seen, had been represented as *indulging in rather a severe habit* of burning Deists with formal solemnity ! O, the inconsistency of heresy ! How are its teachers *tossed to and fro by every wind of doctrine and deceit!* How much to be pitied are the good and confiding *people* who believe, as so much gospel, the *cunningly-devised fables* which these individuals invent, at the expense of truth and of the glorious Church of Christ !

‡ Let the reader note this mildness, and contrast it with the imputed cruelty of this institution. This benevolent act was performed even without the royal sanction.

§ What abominable, hard-hearted people !

greater mildness and humanity can a sensible man require or conceive?

Were this tribunal at all liable to reproach, it would be on account of its clemency; for, even according to the statement of our *traveller*, "the ingredients employed by *Rodriguez* might, in other countries, have insured his passage to the pillory, galleys, or gibbet." Our English *commentator* continues, — " Such punishment," says he, " was quite beneath the dignity of this tribunal. *It would have been much better to punish this wretch in private,* by the meanest constable." It is possible that this Mr. Townsend may have been a very sensible man; but how unavailing is good sense, when opposed by national, and especially religious, prejudice!

It is somewhat singular that a transient foreigner should undertake to pass his severe censure upon the criminal jurisprudence of an illustrious, enlightened nation, and arrogantly dictate to it the propriety of inflicting private rather than public punishment.* If the Inquisition had ordered even one

---

* Pity that England did not take the hint from this great politician. He reminds us of those speculating tourists, (I shall not use the appropriate term,) who visit foreign countries, and have just brains enough to collect or fabricate base falsehoods of the people of whom they write. They are almost sure to swell their tours into two volumes, for the *instruction* of their countrymen, and *not*, of course, for their own pecuniary advantage. How has America been treated by such English scribbling defamers! How have Catholic nations been calumniated, both by English and American Protestants!

For shame! *Prejudice* — still more hideous under the mask of religion; whether " *orthodox* " or heterodox, it is the *same* — hide your deformity; never again contaminate society with your unholy presence, until you have *reformed* your own heart, and atoned for your transgressions " in sackcloth and ashes." — *Translator.*

stripe to be laid on the shoulders of this culprit, *in private*, our sapient traveller would undoubtedly have written a long diatribe upon *such* atrocity, and enriched his *book* of travels with a *striking* picture, where would be seen two sturdy executioners whipping off the flesh of the unfortunate *Rodriguez* in a corner of a frightful dungeon, in presence of some Dominican friars! What right has an itinerant stranger,* who is perfectly ignorant of the cause, to decide why the great tribunal of Spain ought to conceal, or publish, the nature of the crimes, and the degree of notoriety which this horrid woman had given them? In Spain, as elsewhere, government well understands what ought, or ought not, to be made known to the public.

The other *compliments* which this writer pays to the tribunal of the Inquisition are equally shallow and destitute of foundation. "This tribunal *can summon before it whomsoever it pleases, and arrest persons in their very beds at the midnight hour,*" &c. If this traveller alludes to witnesses, he shows his gross ignorance of criminal jurisprudence; for if any thing can reflect honor upon a government, and demonstrate its impartiality and power, it is the authority which it gives its tribunals to bring before them every person, without exception, to depose in relation to the case in question. We read that, some time ago, the chancellor of the exchequer in England

---

* How few of this, or the *missionary* family are even acquainted with the language of the people whose customs they traduce!

was obliged to appear before a judge of a criminal court, and give in his testimony.

He was harassed by questions and cross examinations, and he felt, on the whole, rather uncomfortable.* Our critic would undoubtedly, on that occasion, have exclaimed, — "*Here the tribunal of justice can, when it thinks proper, oblige all to come before it. Happy England! holy liberty!*"

But when the scene lies in Spain, this same individual alters his tone: principles must be altered; justice must be called injustice; and then he cries out, — "THE HOLY OFFICE *can at pleasure oblige all, without any exception, to come forward and testify. Vile and unfortunate Spain! Base compound of despotism and iniquity!*"

Should he, however, allude to persons who are accused of crime, he appears in a still more ridiculous light. Why should not the accused, whoever he may be, be summoned, or arrested, according to circumstances? Singular indeed would be the privilege he would enjoy, that should screen him from the arm of justice. But what particularly shocks the sensitive nerves of his Protestant reverence is, *that the accused can be arrested by night, and even in his bed.* Such, then, is the crying sin of the Inquisition! A debtor, or person guilty of some slight offence, may not, *perhaps*, be arrested at

---

* *Pitt* was reluctantly compelled to appear as evidence, in a celebrated case in London, and doled out his testimony in as costive and equivocal a manner as he possibly could.

midnight, and in his comfortable bed; but will that same person, accused of a capital offence, be equally protected, by the darkness of the night and his enchanted castle, from the ministers of justice? Were he so — which I am very far from believing — I should only say, *so much the worse for England;* and I see no reason why Spain should, so far, respect the *sweet* repose of crime?

We have already noticed the inquisitorial apparatus which was brought into action in the course of a *terrible* AUTO DA FE on the 9th of May, 1764, by virtue of which an infamous criminal was *condemned* to *feast* upon *wine and biscuit* in the public streets of Madrid! It may not be uninstructive to ascertain from his Protestant reverence, Mr. Townsend, the words which the grand inquisitor uttered, when he informed the condemned *Rodriguez* of the sentence which the holy office had pronounced against him: " My son," observed this *holy executioner*, " you are now about to hear the statement of your crimes, and the punishment which must expiate them. Mercy is our favorite and invariable practice. The holy office ever feels a deeper interest in the real reformation than in the punishment of the offender. Let the reproach of your conscience, rather than the penalty which you are now about to undergo, serve you as a source of sorrow and future amendment."*

---

* Mr. Townsend here remarks that *this exhortation might have been made in the same tone and strain of mildness, had the culprit been condemned to the flames.* (Ibid.) Is there any thing surprising

Our Protestant traveller continues: "The very nobility and all the ladies of the court had been invited to witness this ceremony by the Marchioness *Cogolludo*, who afterwards gave a gala to the judges and officers of the Inquisition."

A man, upon the perusal of this transaction, might be surprised, if indeed he could be surprised at any thing of this kind, to find this minister of the holy gospel concluding his narrative with this reflection, viz., "*Had the king wished to destroy this tribunal, and determined to render it despicable in the eyes of his subjects, he could not have adopted a more efficient measure.*" Thus it is that this admirable alliance of legal severity and Christian charity, the harmonizing sympathies of the judges and people, the paternal exhortation of the inquisitor, the very sentence of the court, so well calculated to inspire a moral reformation, the nature of the *punishment*, immediately succeeded by a gala, in whose innocent and elegant amusements the high-toned, noble-minded court of Spain and its enlightened judges so freely shared, and the mild, *unique*, and characteristic jurisprudence of the nation, are totally disregarded, for they *will* not interest the feelings of a spectator, whose eyes, as well as soul, are vitiated by national prejudice, and who will see but one object

---

in this? *Justice*, however isolated, has no necessity for clothing herself in anger. Why should she not experience a transition from unruffled calmness, to parental tenderness, especially when she is under the influence of *Mercy?*

in, and feel contempt for, a scene which should excite the admiration even of a Hindoo, or Mussulman, if acquainted with all the circumstances of the case. Enough, sir, has been laid before a gentleman of your good sense, to form a correct idea of the origin, nature, real character, and mode of proceeding, of the Inquisition; but what truly deserves notice is the fact that this tribunal, calumniated as it has been by ignorance and prejudice, is, in reality, a *court of equity*, which is at least as necessary in the criminal as in the civil department of state.

Grotius gave an excellent definition of equity when he called it "*a remedy for a case to which the law, owing to its deficiency, does not extend.*" * Man can make only general laws, and even so they are in their very nature somewhat unjust, inasmuch as they cannot comprehend every case. *The exception to the rule* is, therefore, precisely as just as the rule itself; and wherever there be not a dispensation, exception, or mitigation, there must necessarily be a violation of the law; because, if the consciences of all once allow an exception to be made, the passions of each will strenuously endeavor to generalize and explain away the law, and eventually destroy it. In the criminal department, this prerogative is commonly reserved to the sovereign, or executive; and hence, pardon, commutations of punishment, *lettres*

---

* Correctio ejus in quo lex propter universalitatem deficit.
Grot. de Jure Belli et Pacis.

de cachet, and sumptuary orders emanate from him. Common experience tells us that the union of the executive and the judiciary must be dangerous in the extreme. I am far from being averse to the executive exercising the divine prerogative of pardon; but then solid discretion should be his guide, otherwise this privilege may and must be productive of the most disastrous consequences. I do believe that, should a question arise, not relative to *pardon*, properly so termed, but to a certain *management* which is not easily defined, and especially in cases which involve religion and public morals, the *redeeming* power would be much more safely vested in an experienced tribunal at once royal and ecclesiastical, as far as the quality of the judges may be concerned.*

I even venture to believe that it is impossible to conceive any thing better than thus to introduce the *oil of mercy* into the creaking and grating hinges of criminal jurisprudence. The Inquisition can, in this point of view, render essential service to society. Madrid will long remember the history of an abominable woman, who had there imposed upon thousands, under the garb of heroic piety, but who was a hypocrite of the deepest dye. Her fictitious director and real accomplice was a monk still more

---

* We are forcibly struck with the wisdom of this remark, on taking a view of the *Spanish* nation. Her prophylactic laws threw around her a formidable ægis against the horrid manœuvres of Calvinism and Lutheranism, which have drowned so many sister nations in a revolutionary tide of blood. The above remark, however, cannot possibly apply to Protestant ascendency. Witness Henry VIII., the *Virgin* Queen, &c. &c.— *Translator*.

wicked than herself. Even the bishop himself was duped by the Satanic ingenuity of this woman, who pretended that a peculiar sickness had confined her to her bed, and from her apparent sanctity obtained, through the unsuspecting and benevolent bishop, a special privilege from the pope to keep the holy eucharist in her chamber. Some time after, it was understood that this very chamber had been perverted into a theatre of licentiousness!

It finally came to the ears of the Inquisition, who had then, if ever, a fair opportunity of getting up an *auto da fe* against these two criminals, and particularly, against the sacrilegious monk. *Justice* could not, even on this occasion, entirely suppress the power of *mercy*.

The Inquisition secretly banished the female culprit, punished her accomplice, *without*, however, *putting him to death*, and saved the reputation of the charitable and generous prelate who had been thus duped.

The case of two Spanish ecclesiastics (*questas*) is well known in the place where the scene occurred. These brothers having had the misfortune to displease a celebrated courtier, were delivered up to the Inquisition, and accused in an indictment which was so artfully drawn up, and supported by such power and influence, as to leave no room to hope for their acquittal. Every engine which iniquity could devise had been resorted to for the destruction of these gentlemen.

However, the inquisitor of Valladolid detected the scheme, and all the seductions of the court could not move him from his post, nor extort from him an unrighteous decision. He now suspected the testimony, exposed its perfidy, and finally pronounced sentence in favor of the prisoners.

An appeal, notwithstanding, was made to the supreme tribunal of the Inquisition at Madrid; the grand inquisitor manfully maintained the cause of justice, quashed the proceedings, and innocence thus triumphed over the giant offspring of patronage and power.

One of the brothers was restored to liberty, and the other, who had escaped, afterwards returned to his fireside and home. *Aveda*, the grand inquisitor, once visited the prisons of the Inquisition, and there saw some persons who were strangers to him. Having inquired of the keeper who they were, "They are," answered he, "men who have been arrested by government, and sent hither for such and such causes." "*All this*," replied the inquisitor-general, "*has nothing to do with religion;*" and he immediately ordered them to be discharged. Chance threw these anecdotes in my way,* and a thousand more, I doubt not, if they were sufficiently known, might likewise attest the happy influence of the In-

---

* A Spanish gentleman, peculiarly distinguished for his elevated character, and the inflexible probity which had uniformly preserved him in the career of honor and danger during the revolutionary storms of his country, has kindly furnished me with these anecdotes.

quisition, viewed, as it ever must be by the *sensible* and enlightened portion of mankind, as a court of equity, and a measure of sound government and discipline.

It should, in fact, be viewed under these three respective heads; for it sometimes deadens the rude and disproportionate severity of criminal jurisprudence; it also places sovereignty in the situation of exercising, with the least possible inconvenience, a certain mode of justice which, under some form or other, is found in every country; and, finally, more successfully than the tribunals of other nations, and in the most salutary manner for the state, it represses immorality, by threatening it, when it assumes a bold and dangerous aspect, to remove the line of demarkation that separates sin from crime. I by no means doubt that a tribunal of this description, adapted to the times, places, and characters, of nations, would be highly useful in every country: that it has been of essential service to Spain, and that its illustrious inhabitants ascribe to it immortal gratitude and praise, is a fact which, I trust, no sensible or moral man can possibly question, after the perusal of my next letter.

I am, sir, &c. &c.

Moscow, 27th *July*, 1815.

LETTER IV.

Sir,

In natural science we constantly read of *mean* quantities; we speak of *mean distance, mean velocity, mean time,* &c. &c. It may, perhaps, be high time to introduce this idea into politics, and to conclude that the best institutions are not those which afford its members the greatest possible degree of happiness for a given time, but rather those that furnish the greatest possible quantum of happiness to the greatest possible number of generations. Such is the *mean happiness;* and I am satisfied that there would be no great difficulty in ascertaining such a point. According to such an axiom, I would be curious to know what answer the most unrelenting enemy to the Inquisition could make to a Spaniard, who (to say nothing about what you have hitherto read on this subject) would justify it in the following manner: —

"You are purblind. Your sphere of vision is extremely limited: it rests upon a single point. Our legislators stand upon a mountain top, and take an immense survey. In the beginning of the sixteenth century, they beheld Europe sending forth her dark and dismal columns of smoke, which portended a universal conflagration; to guard against its desolating rage, they threw up an impenetrable barrier. They resorted to the Inquisition; they used this political means to secure religious unity, and prevent religious wars. You never dreamed of so salutary, so preservative, a design. Let us examine the consequences; experience alone shall be the judge.

"Reflect upon the *thirty years' war*, which the horrid and blasphemous tenets of Luther had kindled throughout Europe; the frightful and infamous excesses in which Baptists, Anabaptists,* the rabble of

---

* The inexhaustible womb of the *reformation* daily gave birth to moral monsters, whose object it was to *improve* upon each other's ungodliness, by devising ways and means to tear up society, and annihilate the religion of the living God. Muncer, Storck, and Stubner, deserted the wicked heresiarch Luther, and *set up for themselves*, upon the disorganizing principle and blasphemous pretext which induced *him* to apostatize from the *pillar and ground of Catholic truth*. They alleged that Luther's doctrine was not sufficiently *pure*. This no man of sense could ever doubt; and happy would it have been for them and their deluded and deluding disciples had they then reëntered the "one fold" from which they strayed. But no; the religion of Heaven was not their favorite object. Plunder, power, and lust, were the deities they *passionately* adored, and enormous were the exactions for the support of such idols. Yes, these monsters prostituted the oracles of God, interpreted them with the venomous tongue of the basilisk and asp, and maintained *their* "ORTHODOXY" with fire and sword: they adopted no other rule of faith or conduct than the Bible; but the destructive consequences of such a measure (for it was not the first time that the *ignorant and unstable*, as well as the wicked, *wrested the Scriptures to their own perdition*) should have taught them, as also the fanatics or impostors of a subsequent date, the absurdity and sanguinary horrors of such an adoption. They sallied forth, held their *meetings*, and Baptists, Anabaptists, Private or General Dunkers, Kethians, Mennonites, Sabbatarians, Uckewallists, &c. &c., as they were, they now cried down the salutary and established laws of church and state. They proclaimed to their *pure and pious* listeners that all things should be in common; that the Spirit of God was their guide; that the magisterial office was not only unlawful, but an encroachment upon their spiritual liberty; that every distinction of birth, or wealth, or rank, was ungodly, and

the Netherlands, had rioted: look at the civil wars of France,* England, and Flanders; the massacre

---

should therefore be abolished; that, as neither the laws of nature nor the precepts of the gospel imposed any restriction upon mankind concerning the number of wives each man should marry, they were entitled to use the liberty which the patriarchs themselves had been allowed! Such licentiousness was greedily seized, and readily adopted by the mob, who were shortly to become members of an earthly kingdom, in which *all should reign* in perfect bliss after they should have exterminated the "ungodly," who were, of course, all those, and especially the good old Catholics, that would not become members of this "*thorough-godly*" community! They trampled upon the sacraments, and the external worship of our holy religion, condemned infant baptism, and rebaptized the new elect! Hence the name of *Anabaptist*. Such monstrous doctrine was propagated throughout a vast portion of unfortunate Germany, and "the kingdom" was soon extended into the Low Countries, which were desolated by the blood of the Catholic clergy and civil magistrates by such impious plunderers, those worse than Gothic tyrants. What wars and wickedness, cruelty and impiety, has not the *reformation* heresy occasioned in the world!— *Translator.*

* "Conde and Coligni, with their Huguenots, had stirred up a formidable civil war in France. '*Good* Queen Bess's' ambassador at that court stimulated and assisted the rebels to the utmost of her power. At last, Vidame, an agent of Conde and Coligni, came *secretly* over to England to negotiate for military, naval, and pecuniary assistance. They succeeded with '*good* Bess,' who, wholly disregarding the solemn treaties by which she was bound to Charles IX., king of France, entered into a formal treaty with the French rebels to send them an army and money, for the purpose of carrying on war against their sovereign, of whom she was *an ally*, having bound herself, in that character, by a *solemn oath on the Evangelists!* By this treaty she engaged to furnish men, ships, and money; and the traitors, on their part, engaged to put Havre de Grace at once into her hands, as a pledge, not only for the repayment of the money to be advanced, but for the restoration of Calais! This infamous compact richly deserved the consequences that attended it.

"The French ambassador in London, when he found that an intercourse was going on between the queen and the agents of the rebels, went to Cecil, the secretary of state, carrying the treaty of Cateau Cambresis in his hand, and demanded, agreeably to the stipulations of that treaty, that the agents of the rebels should be delivered up as traitors to their sovereign; and he warned the English government that any act of aggression, on its part, would annihilate its claim to the recovery of Calais at the end of the eight years. But '*good* Bess' had caused the civil wars in France; she had, by her bribes, and other underhand means, stirred them up, and she believed that the successes of the French rebels were necessary to

on St. Bartholemew's* day, the slaughter at Merindal and Cevennes, the villanous murder of poor

---

her own security on her throne of doubtful right; and, as she hoped to get Calais in this perfidious way, she saw nothing but gain in the perfidy.

"The rebels were in possession of DIEPPE, ROUEN, HAVRE DE GRACE, and had extended their power over a considerable part of Normandy. They at once put HAVRE and DIEPPE into the hands of the English. So infamous and treacherous a proceeding roused the Catholics of France, who now became ashamed of that inactivity, which had suffered a sect, less than a *hundredth part* of the population, to sell their country under the blasphemous plea of a *love of the gospel*. 'Good Bess,' with her usual mixture of hypocrisy and effrontery, sent her proclamations into Normandy, declaring that she meant *no hostility* against her 'good *brother*' the king of France; but merely to protect his Protestant subjects against the tyranny of the *house of Guise*; and that her 'good brother' ought to be *grateful* to her for the assistance she was lending! This cool and hypocritical insolence added fury to the flame. All France could not but recollect that it was the skilful, the gallant, the patriotic duke of Guise who had, only five years before, ejected the English from Calais, their last hold in France; and they now saw these 'sons of the gospel,' as they had the audacity to call themselves, bring those same English back-again, and put two French seaports into their hands at once! Are we to wonder at the inextinguishable hatred of the people of France against this traitorous sect? Are we to wonder that they felt a desire to extirpate the whole of so infamous a race, who had already sold their country to the utmost of their power?"

COBBETT's (*a Protestant*) *Hist. of Reformation.*

* "Though the massacre of ST. BARTHOLOMEW took place in France, yet it has formed so fertile a source of calumny against the religion of our fathers; it has served as a pretence with Protestant historians to justify or palliate so many atrocities on the part of their divers sects; and the queen of England and her ministers had so great a hand in first producing it, and then in punishing Catholics under pretence of avenging it, — that it is necessary for me to give an account of it.

"The Calvinistic Coligni, this pretended saint, basely caused that gallant and patriotic nobleman, the duke of Guise, to be assassinated. But in assassinating this nobleman the wretch did not take off the whole of his family. There was a SON left to avenge that father, and the just vengeance of this son the treacherous Coligni had yet to feel. Peace had taken place between the French king and his rebellious subjects; but Coligni had all along discovered that his treacherous designs only slept. The king was making a progress through the kingdom about four years after the pacification; a plot was formed by Coligni and his associates to kill or seize him; but, by riding fourteen hours without getting off his horse, and without food or drink, he escaped, and got safe to Paris. Another civil war soon broke out, followed by another pacification; but such had been the barbarities committed on both sides, that there could be, and there was, no real forgiveness. The Protestants had been full as sanguinary as the Catholics; and, which has been remarked even by their own historians, their conduct was frequently, not to say uniformly, characterized by plundering, and by hypocrisy and perfidy, unknown to their enemies.

" During this pacification, Coligni had, by the deepest dissimulation, endeavored to worm himself into favor with the young king; and, upon the occasion of a marriage between the king's sister and the young king of Navarre, (afterwards the famous Henry IV.,) Coligni, who, Conde being now dead, was become the chief of his sect, came to Paris, with a company of his Protestant adherents, to partake in the celebration, and that, too, at the king's invitation. After he had been there a day or two, some one shot at him, in the street, with a blunderbuss, and wounded him in two or three places, but not dangerously. His partisans ascribed this to the young duke of Guise, though no proof has ever been produced in support of the assertion. They, however, got about their leader, and threatened revenge, as was very natural. Taking this for the ground of their justification, the court resolved to anticipate the blow; and, on Sunday, the 24th of August, 1572, it being ST. BARTHOLOMEW's day, they put their design in execution. There was great difficulty in prevailing upon the young king to give his consent; but, at last, by the representation and entreaties of his mother, those of the duke of Anjou, his brother, and those of the duke of Guise, he was prevailed upon. The dreadful orders were given; at the appointed moment the signal was made; the duke of Guise, with a band of followers, rushed to and broke open the house of Coligni, whose dead body was soon thrown out of the window into the street. The people of Paris, who mortally hated the Protestants, and who could not have forgotten Coligni's having *put the English in possession of Dieppe and Havre;* who could not have forgotten that, while the old enemy of France was thus again brought into the country of Coligni and his Protestants, this same traitor and his sect had basely assassinated that brave nobleman, the late duke of Guise, who had driven the English from their last hold, Calais, and who had been assassinated at the very moment when he was endeavoring to drive this old enemy from Havre, into which this Coligni and his sect had brought that enemy;—the people of Paris could not but remember these things, and, remembering them, they could not but hold Coligni and his sect in detestation indescribable. Besides this, there were few of them, some one or more of whose relations had not perished, or suffered in some way or other, from the plunderings or butcheries of these marauding and murdering Calvinists, whose creed taught them that good works were unavailing, and that no deeds, however base or bloody, could bar their way to salvation. These 'Protestants,' as they were called, bore no more resemblance to Protestants of the present day than the wasp bears a resemblance to the bee. That name then was, and it was justly, synonymous with *banditti*;

that is, *robber and murderer;* and the persons bearing it had been, by becoming the willing tool of every ambitious rebel, a greater scourge to France than foreign war, pestilence, and famine, united.

"Considering these things, and taking into view that the people, always ready to suspect, even beyond the limits of reason, heard the cry of '*treason*' on all sides, is it any wonder that they fell upon the followers of Coligni, and that they spared none of the sect that they were able to destroy? When we consider these things, and especially when we see the son of the assassinated duke of Guise lead the way, is it not a most monstrous violation of truth to ascribe this massacre to the *principles of the Catholic religion?* With equal justice might we ascribe the act of BELLINGHAM (who sent for his *Church Prayer Book* the moment he was lodged in Newgate) *to the principles of the Church of England*. No one has ever been base and impudent enough to do this; why, then, are there men so base and impudent as to ascribe this French massacre to *Catholic principles?*

"The massacre of Paris very far exceeded the wishes of the court; and orders were instantly despatched to the great towns in the provinces to prevent similar scenes. Such scenes took place, however, in several places; but though, by some Protestant writers, the whole number of persons killed has been made to amount to a *hundred thousand,* an account, published in 1582, and made up from accounts *collected from the ministers of the different towns,* made the number, for all France, amount to only 786 persons! Dr. LINGARD, (Note T. vol. v.) with his usual fairness, says, 'if we *double* this number, we shall not be far from the real amount.' The Protestant writers began at 100,000; then fell to 70,000; then to 30,000; then to 20,000; then to 15,000; and, at last, to 10,000!—all in *round* numbers! One of them, in an hour of great indiscretion, ventured upon obtaining returns of *names* from the ministers themselves; and then out came the 786 persons in the whole!

"A number truly horrible to think of; but a number not half so great as that of those English Catholics whom '*good* Queen Bess' had, even at this time, (the fourteenth year of her reign,) caused to be *ripped up, racked till the bones came out of their sockets,* or caused to be despatched, or to die in prison or in exile; and this, too, observe, not for rebellions, treasons, robberies, and assassinations, like those of Coligni and his followers, but simply and solely for adhering to the religion of their and their fathers, which religion she had openly practised for years, and to which religion she had most solemnly sworn that she sincerely belonged! The annals of hypocrisy, conjoined with impudence, afford nothing to equal her behavior upon the occasion of the ST. BARTHOLOMEW. She was daily racking people nearly to death to get *secrets* from them; she was daily ripping the bowels out of women, as well as men, for saying or hearing that *mass* for the celebration of which the churches of England had been erected; she was daily *mutilating, racking,* and *butchering* her own innocent and conscientious subjects; and yet she, and her profligate court women, when the French ambassador came with the king of France's explanation of the cause of the massacre, received him in *deep mourning,* and with all the marks of disapprobation. But, when she remonstrated with her 'good brother,' the king of France,

A ship of the line could float in the blood which heretical innovation had caused to flow.

" The Inquisition would have shed but its own. It is you, presumptuous and ignorant revilers, who, in your infuriate blindness, have buried Europe in blood. Well, indeed, does it become you to blame our Spanish kings for having foreseen and prevented

---

writers make it their theme of illiberal declamation. The exertion of authority, made by a sovereign in defence of the laws and constitution of his kingdom against rebellion, is no other than the exercise of a just and lawful power, which no prudent man will venture to question or condemn. If, in the execution, abuses were committed, they are to be lamented. Those abuses will always be of less pernicious consequence to the public than the outrages of civil war. The country was brought back to a state of tranquillity, when the intrigues of the prince of Orange threw it back into rebellion. From the Huguenot camp in France, he maintained a correspondence with the Calvinists in Holland; by his emissaries and preachers in disguise, he diffused a spirit of revolt through the country, granted military commissions in his own name, and from all who betrayed any disaffection to the Catholic religion, or to the Spanish government, he collected voluntary contributions to defray the expense of his intended operations.

" When the plot was ripe for execution, the insurgents suddenly assembled in great force, and gained several advantages, before the duke of Alva had any suspicion of their machinations, or could make head against them. The years 1570, 1571, and 1572, are marked with the progress they made in their rebellious enterprise; several towns in Holland and Zealand, where the *reformers* chiefly prevailed, joined their standard. The victories of the Protestants were sullied by that savage ferocity which spends itself equally upon the defenceless monk as upon the armed soldier. They listened not to the dictates of humanity or religion, but promiscuously tore in pieces every thing that fell in their way. (*Watson, Hist. of Spain,* vol. i. b. 7.) In rebellions, lenity is seldom shown, while fierce revenge steels the heart on one side, and severe justice whets the sword on the other. Success gave the prince of Orange an absolute power to regulate every thing he pleased in the towns he was master of, but political considerations made him cautious not to show that power: with seeming deference he affected to consult the states, and to have their sanction for all he chose to do. By him the exercise of the Catholic religion was banished from the churches, and the only worship publicly allowed was the Protestant, as taught by Calvin, and practised in Geneva and the Palatinate." — This was an Inquisition with a vengeance! — *Reeve's Church History.*

of Charles I.,* of the Prince of Orange,† &c. &c.

nate prince. He was badly qualified to counteract the plots, or put down the conspiracies, of the Huguenot faction; and dearly did he and all France suffer for it. At a meeting of the States-General at Blois, in 1576, he granted peace to the Calvinists on terms the most favorable to them. This, however, did not satisfy them. In the year 1580, they further obtained an edict of pacification, whereby they were allowed additional privileges. Henry, instead of consulting for the happiness of his nation, or the security of religion, gave himself up to luxury and debauch. The enemies seized the opportunity, and finally despatched their king, to make way for their favorite Henry, king of Navarre, afterwards Henry IV. of France.

The Calvinists first murdered a Dominican friar, of the name of James Clement; and one of them, dressing himself in the monastic robes of the deceased, murdered the monarch. The Huguenot faction, in *their usual charity and love for their Catholic neighbors*, imputed the crime to their victim, whom they had previously assassinated!—See the *Dissertations of Frederick Steill and Matthew Dolmans.*

* What may not have been expected from Scotland, when she sacrificed her Catholicity and her independence to the evil spirit of Calvinism upon the altar of the *reformation!* She of course became selfish, mercenary, and mean. Her avarice commenced with the plunder of the temples of the Most High, and terminated with a somewhat Judas-like act of perfidy *in betraying and selling her royal master for a few pieces of silver!* She delivered up the unfortunate Charles to the ferocious cabal of a Calvinistic parliament, and the parricide Cromwell and his banditti next beheaded him on the scaffold. What misery has not Protestantism caused to Scotland and England!—*Translator.*

† "Margaret, duchess of Parma, a natural daughter of Charles V., was governess of the Low Countries, under Philip of Spain. In this disturbed state of his Flemish dominions, Philip judged a female hand too weak to guide the helm of government through the swelling tide of rebellion. Military force became a necessary evil. The duke of Alva had orders to repair from Italy to the Netherlands, and to reduce the rebels to obedience. He arrived with a powerful army in 1568. William, the prince of Orange, headed the Calvinist insurgents; the Belgic plains were drenched with blood. The prince was too weak to stand the contest for any long time. He disbanded his troops, and retired into Germany, till a favorable opportunity should offer for renewing his hostile operations. Alva, in the interim, exerted the utmost severity in bringing the state offenders to public justice. Whether he exceeded the powers of his commission, or whether he wantonly indulged a natural disposition to cruelty or revenge, of which he is accused, or whether, in fine, the Spanish monarch himself pursued the most prudent means of regaining the good-will of his revolted subjects, is a matter of opinion; party

A ship of the line could float in the blood which heretical innovation had caused to flow.

" The Inquisition would have shed but its own. It is you, presumptuous and ignorant revilers, who, in your infuriate blindness, have buried Europe in blood. Well, indeed, does it become you to blame our Spanish kings for having foreseen and prevented

---

writers make it their theme of illiberal declamation. The exertion of authority, made by a sovereign in defence of the laws and constitution of his kingdom against rebellion, is no other than the exercise of a just and lawful power, which no prudent man will venture to question or condemn. If, in the execution, abuses were committed, they are to be lamented. Those abuses will always be of less pernicious consequence to the public than the outrages of civil war. The country was brought back to a state of tranquillity, when the intrigues of the prince of Orange threw it back into rebellion. From the Huguenot camp in France, he maintained a correspondence with the Calvinists in Holland; by his emissaries and preachers in disguise, he diffused a spirit of revolt through the country, granted military commissions in his own name, and from all who betrayed any disaffection to the Catholic religion, or to the Spanish government, he collected voluntary contributions to defray the expense of his intended operations.

" When the plot was ripe for execution, the insurgents suddenly assembled in great force, and gained several advantages, before the duke of Alva had any suspicion of their machinations, or could make head against them. The years 1570, 1571, and 1572, are marked with the progress they made in their rebellious enterprise; several towns in Holland and Zealand, where the *reformers* chiefly prevailed, joined their standard. The victories of the Protestants were sullied by that savage ferocity which spends itself equally upon the defenceless monk as upon the armed soldier. They listened not to the dictates of humanity or religion, but promiscuously tore in pieces every thing that fell in their way. (*Watson, Hist. of Spain*, vol. i. b. 7.) In rebellions, lenity is seldom shown, while fierce revenge steels the heart on one side, and severe justice whets the sword on the other. Success gave the prince of Orange an absolute power to regulate every thing he pleased in the towns he was master of, but political considerations made him cautious not to show that power : with seeming deference he affected to consult the states, and to have their sanction for all he chose to do. By him the exercise of the Catholic religion was banished from the churches, and the only worship publicly allowed was the Protestant, as taught by Calvin, and practised in Geneva and the Palatinate." — This was an Inquisition with a vengeance ! — *Reeve's Church History.*

all this. Tell us not that the Inquisition has been guilty of various abuses at various times; such is not the question; for the real, the only, object of the inquiry is, to know whether, for the last three centuries, the Inquisition has insured more peace and happiness in Spain than were in all the countries of Europe put together. To sacrifice the positive to the problematic happiness of future generations may be the visionary calculation of a philosopher, but *legislators* would adopt a different course. Even were not this decisive observation sufficient, the passing events of the present time would speak volumes in my favor, and must strike you dumb.

"The Inquisition not only saved, but has immortalized, the kingdom of Spain. It preserved and invigorated the national spirit, the faith and religious patriotism which produced all the prodigies you have already witnessed, and which, according to every appearance, by preserving Spain, have saved all Europe by a policy at once the most noble and uncompromising. From the heights of the Pyrenees the Inquisition frowned down upon the monster Philosophism, which had every reason to hate it, and to tremble. With sleepless caution it watched the numerous *volumes* of infidelity which rolled from the mountains with all the destructive fury of the avalanche. Such of them, however, as eluded the power and vigilance of this tribunal were sufficient to insure for the *usurper* such subjects as were *worthy* of him, while the great mass of the nation remained loyal and true to their country and God; the Inquisition alone could restore them to their lawful sovereign, in the same condition as they were when it had the misfortune of being deprived of them."

It is impossible, sir, to give a *reasonable* answer to such observations; but what is very extraordinary and very little known, as I presume, is the satisfactory and triumphant apology which the impious Voltaire himself has made in favor of the Inquisition, and which I shall now lay before you, as a lasting monument of the good sense which can discriminate facts, and of the passion which *will not* see their true and genuine cause.

"In Spain," says he, "during the sixteenth and seventeenth centuries, there were none of those bloody revolutions, conspiracies, and cruel punishments, which were seen in the other courts of Europe. Neither did the duke of Lermo nor Count Olivares shed the blood of their enemies on the scaffold. Her kings were not assassinated, as were those of France; neither were they brought to the block, as were those of England.* *In a word, were we to except the horrors of the Inquisition*, Spain would have been irreproachable." †

---

* Had Voltaire lived long enough to witness the disgraceful but unmerited fate of the unfortunate *Louis*, and his amiable consort, *Marie Antoinette*, he might have altered this expression, which could run thus: "*Her kings were not assassinated, neither did they die under the hands of the common executioner, as was the case in England and France.*"

† Essay on General History, t. iv. chap. 177, p. 135. Œuvres Completes, in 8vo. t. xix.

When Voltaire said that *the Spanish nation would have been faultless, had it not been for the horrors of the Inquisition, which, however, alone preserved it from the horrid calamities that disgraced the other kingdoms of Europe*, he evidently showed how much he was influenced by prejudice, and a hatred of order and religion. To me, sir, it is a real satisfaction to see a wicked genius thus chastised, and condemned to have recourse to absurdity and folly itself, as a self-punishment for wilful error. I am less delighted at his natural superiority than his very nothingness, when he thus forgets his high destination. After the tragic scenes which Europe has witnessed, and in which she sustained so painful a part, how great must be the effrontery that would inculpate Spain for an institution which would have effectually prevented such indescribable calamities, had it been adopted by those countries that became the theatres of bloodshed!

"Had the holy office instituted even sixty suits in a century, it would have saved the awful sight of a heap of human bodies which could exceed the height of the Alps, and stop the rapid course of the Rhine and the Po."* But of all the nations of Europe it least becomes France, as well as England, to comment upon the Inquisition, after the evils which each has caused in the world, and still con-

---

* Anonymous author of a work entitled, "Qu'importe aux Pretres?" Christiapople, 1797, in 8vo. p. 192.

tinues to inflict upon itself. How inexcusable must be the malicious ridicule thrown upon Spain for her wisdom in adopting an institution which has so fortunately preserved her! Justice ought to be done to that illustrious nation. She is in the small minority of those countries on the European continent that have not been accomplices in the abominable revolution of France. She, it is true, finally became its victim, but the blood of four hundred thousand foreigners has more than sufficiently avenged her; and we now behold her readopting her ancient maxims, with a degree of ardor which merits the respect of the universe, however willing its enemies may be to exaggerate and falsify. Even the committee of the Cortes, to whom I have frequently alluded, were convinced of the advantages of the Inquisition, when they reflected upon the desolating evils it had prevented. To extricate themselves, however, from their dilemma; the reporter of that body had recourse to an ingenious and, as he supposed, a happy expedient, which was to deny such an influence to this tribunal, and ascribe it to a different cause! "*If the authority of the bishops,*" said he, "*could have been preserved, it would have been of service to Spain, by defending her against the late heresiarchs. It is not to the Inquisition that we are indebted for this happiness.*" *

---

* *Por que no se debe attribuir a la Inquisicion la felicidad que ha gozada España de no ser alterada por los ultimos heresiarchas.*

How prejudice bewilders the sense of man! What little regard has he for what he utters, when hurried along by hatred or passion! We have seen, in the second letter, that the Spanish bishops, so far from complaining of the inquisitors, viewed them, on the contrary, as *faithful allies* in the preservation of the faith. But, granting all to the committee, to refute it by its very words, if the ordinary power of the bishops were sufficient for Spain to drive back the *demon of the north*, how could this same power, usurped by the Inquisition, and *increased and modified* in a very attractive manner, be of no benefit to Spain? It is a well-known fact that the heresiarchs of the *reformation* could never obtain a foothold in Spain, for which, of course, some cause should have been assigned. What was that *cause*? Not the power of the bishops, for the Inquisition had stripped them of it; neither was it the Inquisition itself, as the committee assure us on their word of honor! Much less can we attribute the cause to the civil tribunals, or governors of provinces; for the Inquisition is, in its very nature, of a civil character, unconnected with, and uninfluenced by, religious concerns. What, then, can be the cause? If the committee have not seen it, it is because they *would* not. There is no man, who will open his eyes to the light of reason and truth, who will not immediately perceive that all the European nations had been more or less attacked and overthrown by the heresiarchs, if we except Spain, and such countries as have more or less adopted the jurisdiction and forms of the Inquisition, and that equity and reason equally deny the preservation of Spain to any other cause than the Inquisition itself, especially when its numerous enemies, equally hostile to order, morality, and religion, cannot possibly trace it to a different source. It is just as if the nations of Europe, scourged, as they were, by a mortal pestilence in the fourteenth century, observed to a sister and neighboring country that had been fortunate enough to escape its ravages, in consequence of a specific remedy which had been acknowledged by all, and which she herself had used with unqualified success, — " We do admit the prophylactic virtue of your specific ; it is most happily adapted to the case, and well calculated to insure your health and prosperity; yet *other remedies*, we suppose, might have answered every purpose." What is more ridiculous? Do we not, in reality, know that, in no other nation of Europe, those *other remedies* had answered, and that they could not have been even found elsewhere?

I should consider myself guilty of an important omission in my apology for the Inquisition, were I not to notice the influence of this institution upon the character of the people. If Spain preserved its principles, unity, and the public spirit which have so long saved her, she is exclusively indebted to the Inquisition for such happiness. Look at the offscourings of mankind, — those beings who were educated in the impious schools of modern philosophism, — what was their conduct in Spain? Evil, nought but evil. They alone called forth tyranny, or *covenanted* with it; they alone have preached up the doctrine of half-measures,* a conformity to circumstances, a degrading timidity, weakness, and procrastination; in a word, they sacrificed every principle, and virtuous and patriotic resistance, to ill-gotten power and human respect. Had Spain been doomed to perish, she would have fallen by this servile and impious system. I am aware, sir, that the common herd, and numbers of those who are *wise in their own conceit*, attribute her preservation to the Cortes! She has, on the contrary, survived, in *spite* of the Cortes, who have given more *trouble* to England than her policy thought proper to reveal. But no, sir; it was the Spanish people who achieved all; and although there had been some Spaniards who joined the *philosophic* faction and the enemies of the Inquisition, yet were they willing to sacrifice their lives for the real good of the nation. What could the people, in their turn, effect, had they not been directed by national feeling, patriotic impressions, and what heretical calumny and ignorance deemed it expedient to call Spanish *superstition?* †

---

* Better known in *our* national legislature by the name of "ride and tie." — *Translutor.*

† The word *superstition* is frequently used in a vague and indefinite sense. Etymologically considered, it may be defined to be an excessive worship offered to the Deity, — *super*, over, or above, and *statio*, a standing. Such a mode of worship is *vicious*, and therefore condemned by the Catholic Church of God. It also denotes a *false* worship, such as the pagans paid to their idols, from

Would you extinguish the enthusiasm which inspires the mind with sublime sentiments, and prompts to noble undertakings? Would you freeze up the dignified current of the heart, and substitute egotism for an ardént love of country, and then rob the people of their faith, and make them philosophists? In all Europe, a people cannot be found who are less known, and more calumniated, than the Spaniards. *Spanish superstition* has passed for a proverb; yet nothing is more false. The enlightened classes of that country are as fully convinced of it as we are. As to the mere people, it is possible that the reverence paid to the saints, or, to speak more strictly, the honor paid to whatever represents them, might now and then exceed the bounds of propriety, but the doctrine of the infallible Church of Christ being once laid down and firmly established on this point, so as to make no room for the slightest plausible cavil, the abuse which may result from it, on the part of the people, is trivial, and is not even without its ad-

---

the foolish impression that a supernatural power resided in them. Heretics are guilty of blasphemy and sin against the Holy Ghost, when they say that the Holy Catholic Church is *idolatrous;* for the Scriptures assure us that He *confirmed* his Church in *all truth,* and that our divine Savior is to remain with her even *unto the end of the world.* How, then, can she be guilty of idolatry or superstition,— crimes which her wisdom and sanctity naturally abhor and anathematize? It also implies that *wicked* worship which sorcerers and magicians pay to the devil instead of God. Ignorance and malice have, from the very birth of the reformation bantling even to the present day, most *impertinently* ridiculed, and treated as superstitious, the worship which is paid to God by religious rites and ceremonies. On the same principle ought the biblical canters to condemn the whole ritual and ceremonial law of Moses, which was prescribed by God himself, as a system of gross superstition! — *Translator.*

vantage, as I could demonstrate, if it were not considered a digression from the main subject. Besides, the Spaniards have less prejudice and less superstition than the people of other nations who mock them, while they are seemingly unconscious of their own.

I expect that you know many very honest and highly-respectable persons who believe in the virtue of amulets, in the existence of ghosts, sympathetic remedies, sorcerers, and witches, as also in dreams, and the like, and who would immediately rise from table, were they, *unfortunately*, to find the number of the company to consist of *twelve*, who would turn pale at the upsetting of a salt-cellar, and who would sooner forfeit a rich inheritance than commence a journey or voyage on a certain day in the week! But, sir, visit Spain, and you will be astonished to find no such degrading superstition.* The reason

---

* To the reflecting mind, uncontaminated by sectarian bigotry, it may not be considered uninteresting to observe that the northern nations of Europe are remarkable for a *cowardly* superstition, for necromancy, and the withering fear of the " wicked principle," while the southern regions are somewhat characterized for a superstition of a more *confidential*, benevolent, and *religious* nature. Such is the fact. May it not, in some measure, be thus explained? The Catholic Church has more uniformly enlightened the latter than the former section of the world. Besides, the ravages and unnatural excesses of a *false* reformation, which fought its way into *established* power, against principle, conviction, morality, and religion in the north, must have occasioned many a qualm of conscience, and given " a local habitation and a name " to a numerous family of the ghostly tribe clothed, as it may be supposed, in terror and in sorrow. Well might the haunted souls of such awe-stricken *reformers* exclaim, with Macbeth, —

> Avaunt! and quit my sight! let the earth hide thee!
> Thy bones are marrowless, thy blood is cold;

is, because the principle of the Catholic religion is essentially contrary to all silly as well as sinful conceits, and Catholicity invariably not only sets her face against them, but endeavors to put them down, wherever she is not oppressed by wicked power, or the *diseased mind* of heretical tyranny. All this I assert without, at the same time, pretending to deny that she has, in this respect, been powerfully aided by the good sense of the Spanish nation. Notwithstanding, as *there must be heresies*, (such is the lamentable perversity of the human heart,) so calumnies, however apparently patriotic and pious they be, will not cease to exist; and we accordingly find that it was stated in the English House of Commons (22d Nov. 1814) *that whatever could have been done in the way of remonstrance and representation to oppose the* shameful *measures of the Spanish authorities, and especially the reëstablishment of the* detest-

---

> Thou hast no speculation in those eyes
> Which thou dost glare with!

> What man dare, I dare:
> Approach thou like the rugged Russian bear,
> The armed rhinoceros, or the Hyrcan tiger —
> Take any shape but that, and my firm nerves
> Shall never tremble; or be alive again
> And dare me to the desert with thy sword:
> If trembling I inhibit thee, *protest* me.

While the voice of the murdered might respond, with the virtuous and patriotic Macduff, —

> O horror! horror! horror! tongue nor heart
> Cannot conceive nor name thee!
> Confusion now hath made its masterpiece:
> Most sacrilegious murder hath broke ope
> The Lord's anointed temple, and stole thence
> The life o' the building.
>   *Translator.*

able *Inquisition, had been attempted, but in vain, by the English ambassador at Madrid.* I assure you, with the utmost candor of soul, and the perfect recollection of what I have already stated, that I cannot possibly detect any thing which can warrant the application of the English epithet "detestable" to a tribunal so righteous, patriotic, and royal. An accusation, however, so solemn and severe, brought forward, as it had been, in presence of the honorable House of Commons, requires a special investigation; and I expect that I shall show, in my subsequent letters, that the English government has *probably* less right than that of any other nation in Europe to upbraid the Inquisition of Spain.

Allow me, in the mean time, to conclude this letter with wishing you

Farewell, &c. &c.

Moscow, Aug. 15, 1815.

LETTER V.

Sir,

You certainly will not be surprised that the attack which has been made upon the Spanish nation, in the very heart of the British parliament, should merit a particular examination. The representatives of Great Britain ought to be clearly understood, when they express their sentiments in their legislative capacity. The English people, undoubtedly the first and most respectable in the large family of Protestantism, are, besides, the only people who have a national voice and the right of speech as a people.* I therefore think it incumbent

---

* We, of course, except the citizens of republican America.

☞ The reader will please to bear in mind that any observations made in the preceding, and which will be found in this and the subsequent, letter, are not intended for the *people*, but the *government*, of Great Britain. As noble, brave, and generous souls as ever lived have been, and still are, found in the Protestant community of Great Britain and Ireland; while the members and the immense *political* army of *that government* are the most unrelenting, tyrannic, and unprincipled, that ever blasted the *green fields* of liberty, or desolated the sanctuary of religion, with the unhallowed fire of heresy. To exhibit, as briefly as the nature of the subject can admit, the deep and deadly hatred of the *reformation* to justice, liberty, and Catholicity, it may not be uninteresting to American freemen to introduce to their notice a few statutes and cases in relation to the manner in which Protestantism became *established* in England, Ireland, and Scotland; which will not only show the iniquity of its birth, and the infamy of its supposed maturity, but also the horrid injustice of taxing the Cath-

upon me, and perhaps useful to them to ask them for *an account of their faith*, while at the same time

---

olic religion with cruelty, and upbraiding Spain for its Inquisition. In 1532, Henry VIII. apostatized from the venerable Church of Christ, and we accordingly find him, in the subsequent year, sending forth his Protestant *bull*, which was as monstrous as that of the tyrant Phalaris. — *Translator.*

HENRY VIII.

1533. "Every person presented, or indicted of any heresy, or duly accused by two lawful witnesses, may be cited, arrested, or taken by an ordinary, or other of the king's subjects, and committed to the ordinary to answer in open court; and, being convict, shall abjure his heresies; and, *refusing so to do, or falling into relapse,* SHALL BE BURNED in open place, for an example to others." (1)

1538. "John Nicholson, a priest, was accused of heresy, for holding an opinion against the bodily presence of Christ; for which he was condemned, had judgment at the king's mouth, and WAS BURNED at Smithfield." (2) *Eodem anno.* Nov. 27, "A man and woman, Dutch Anabaptists, WERE BURNED in Smithfield." (3)

1539. "If any person, by word, writing, &c. &c., do preach, teach, or hold opinions, that, in the blessed sacrament of the altar, under form of bread and wine, after the consecration thereof, there is not present, really, *the natural body and blood of our Savior Jesus Christ ;* or that *in the flesh, under form of bread, is not the very blood of Christ;* or that *with the blood, under the form of wine, is not the very flesh of Christ* — as well apart as if they were both together — then *he shall be adjudged a heretic,* and SUFFER DEATH BY BURNING, and shall *forfeit to the king all his lands, tenements, hereditaments, goods, and chattels, as in case of high treason.*" (4)

"And if any preach, or teach, or obstinately affirm, or defend, that *the communion of the blessed sacrament, in both kinds, is necessary for the health of man's soul,* or should be ministered in both kinds ; or that auricular confession is not expedient and necessary to be used, *he shall be adjudged, suffer death, and forfeit lands and goods as a felon.*" (5)

1539. "In the month of November, Hugh Faringdon, abbot of Reading, and two priests, named Rug and Onion, were HANGED and QUARTERED at READING. The same day was Richard Whiting, abbot of Glastonbury, HANGED and QUARTERED at

---

(1) Pickering's Statutes, vol. iv. p. 279.
(2) Stowe's (*a Protestant*) Chronicles, p. 176.
(3) Idem.
(4) Pickering's Statutes, vol. iv. p. 471.
(5) Idem.

I do so with the respect to which they are entitled. We shall probably see, by judging of the past, that

---

Torre Hill. John Thorne and Roger James, monks, were at the same time EXECUTED; also, shortly after, John Beck, abbot of Colchester, was executed; — *all for denying the king's supremacy.*" (1)

1540. April 10. " Sir William Peterson, priest, late commissary of Calais, and Sir William Richardson, were both DRAWN, HANGED, and QUARTERED in the market-place, *for the supremacy.*" (2)

Eodem anno. "The 29th of April, one named Maundeveld, another named Colens, and one other, were examined in St. Margaret's Church, and WERE CONDEMNED FOR ANABAPTISTS; and were, on the 3rd of May, BURNED *in the highway*, beyond Southwark, towards Newington." (3)

Eodem anno. "July 30, were drawn from the town of London, to West Smithfield, Robert Barnes, D. D., T. Gerard, parson of Huny Lane, and W. Jerom, vicar of Stephen Heath; also Edward Powell, Thomas Able, and Richard Fitherstone, all three doctors. The first three were drawn to a stake, and there BURNED. The other three were drawn to a gallows, and there HANGED, HEADED, and QUARTERED. The three first were executed *for divers heresies*, the others *for denying the king's supremacy.*" (4)

Eodem anno. "The 4th of August, were drawn to Tyburn six persons, and one led between twain, to wit, Lawrence Cooke, Wm. Horne, Giles Horne, Clement Philips, Edmond Brahelme, Darby Gening, and Robert Bird, — all HANGED and QUARTERED, and had been attainted by parliament, *for denial of the king's supremacy.*" (5)

1541. " Sir David Genson was drawn through Southwark, and *there executed for the supremacy.*" (6)

1542—3. "If any spiritual person preach, teach, or maintain any thing, *contrary to the king's instructions or determinations*, MADE, OR TO BE MADE, and shall be thereof convict, he shall, for his first offence, recant; for his second, abjure and bear a fagot; and, for his third, shall be adjudged a heretic, and BE BURNED, *and lose all his goods and chattels.*" (7)

1544. "March 7, Germaine Gardiner, and Larke, parson of Chelsea, were EXECUTED at Tyburn, *for denying the king's supremacy.*" (8)

1546. " Ann Ascue, a young woman of merit as well as beauty, who had great connections with the chief ladies at court, and with the queen herself, was accused of dogmatizing on the delicate article, the

---

(1) Stowe's Chronicles, p. 577.
(2) Idem, p. 579.
(3) Idem, p. 579.
(4) Idem, p. 581.
(5) Stowe's Chronicles, p. 581
(6) Idem. p. 582.
(7) Pickering, vol. v. p. 130.
(8) Stowe's Chronicles, p. 586.

the system best known in England by the name of *toleration*, cannot associate with any *positive* faith.

---

real presence. (1) * * * She was put to the torture in the most barbarous manner. * * * Some authors add an extraordinary circumstance, that the chancellor, who stood by, ordered the lieutenant of the Tower to stretch the rack still farther, but that officer refused compliance. The chancellor menaced him, but met with a new refusal; upon which that magistrate, who was otherwise a person of merit, but intoxicated with religious zeal, put his own hand to the rack, and drew it so violently that *he almost tore her body asunder.* Her constancy still surpassed the barbarity of her persecutors; and they found all their efforts to be baffled. SHE WAS CONDEMNED TO BE BURNED ALIVE; *and, being so dislocated by the rack that she could not stand, she was carried to the stake in a chair.* Together with her were conducted N. Balenian, a priest, J. Lassels, of the king's household, and J. Adams, a tailor, who HAD BEEN CONDEMNED FOR THE SAME CRIME TO THE SAME PUNISHMENT." (2)
THE FOUR WERE BURNT ALIVE.

EDWARD VI.

1551. April 24. "George Paris, a Dutchman, was BURNED IN SMITHFIELD FOR ARIANISM." (3)

1552. "If any person or persons, inhabiting within this realm, or any other his majesty's dominions, shall * * * *willingly and wittingly* HEAR AND BE PRESENT AT *any other manner or form of common prayer*, of administration of the sacraments, of making of ministers in the churches, or of any other rites contained in the book annexed to this act than is mentioned and set forth in the said book, and shall be thereof convicted, he or they *shall suffer imprisonment for six months; for the second offence, imprisonment for one whole year; and for the third offence, imprisonment during his or their lives.*" (4)

JOAN BOACHER, for having denied "that Jesus Christ was truly incarnate of the Virgin," was condemned to the flames. The horrid and hoary-headed sinner, Archbishop Cranmer, whose *rebellious* conduct subsequently sent him to the flames, expostulated with the young Edward, and urged the propriety of his signing the death-warrant of this unfortunate woman. *Lying* Hume, who wishes to laud

---

(1) "The denial of the real presence SUBJECTED THE PERSON TO DEATH BY FIRE, and to the same forfeiture as in cases of treason; and *admitted not the privilege of abjuring* — an unheard-of severity, and *unknown to the Inquisition.*" (a)
(2) Hume's England, vol. ii. p. 442.
(3) Stowe's Chronicles, p. 605.
(4) Pickering's Statutes, vol. iv. p. 350.

(a) Hume's England, vol. ii. p. 403.

England tolerates every sect, but proscribes the religion whose imperishable trunk has shaken off

the promising *saint* of the reformation, makes the apostate Cranmer say to Edward that, —

"There was a great difference between errors on other points of divinity, and those which were in direct contradiction of the Apostles' Creed. *These latter were impieties against God, which the prince, being God's deputy, ought to repress.* Edward, overcome by importunity, at last submitted, although with tears in his eyes; and he told Cranmer that, if any wrong was done, the guilt should lie entirely on his head." (1)
SHE WAS BURNED ALIVE.

ELIZABETH.

The Archbishop Cranmer issued a proclamation, ordering that " all preaching, catechizing, and praying in any family, where any are present besides the family, be utterly extinguished;" "and that none be admitted to preach unless he be ordained according to the manner of the Church of England." (2)

"If a man hears mass but once in his lifetime, upon a second refusal of this oath, [the oath of supremacy,] *he shall be adjudged guilty of high treason*." (3)

"Those not repairing to church every Sunday, shall forfeit twenty pounds for every month they are absent.

"The month here is to be accounted twenty-eight days; so that the recusant will forfeit thirteen score pounds in the year." (4)

"If any above sixteen years of age shall be convicted of absenting himself from church, without lawful cause, one month; impugn the queen's authority in causes ecclesiastical; frequent conventicles, or persuade others so to do, on pretence of exercise of religion, — *he shall be committed to prison until he conforms.*

"If, within three months after such conviction, he refuses to conform, and submit himself, being thereto lawfully required, *he shall, in open assize or sessions, abjure the realm.*

"If the offender refuses to abjure, or returns without the queen's license, he is *guilty of felony without benefit of clergy.*

"The offender who abjures [the realm,] or, on being required, refuses so to do, *forfeits his goods and his lands during life.*" (5)

"The ecclesiastical commissioners, of whom three made a quorum, were directed to make inquiry not only by the legal method of jury and witness, but by all other means they could devise; that is, BY

---

(1) Hume's England, vol. ii. p. 485.
(2) Neal's History of the Puritans, vol. i. p. 348.
(3) Laws against Papists and Popish recusants, nonconformists, and nonjurors, p. 8.
(4) Idem, p. 12.
(5) Idem, p. 18.

many a worthless and ruinous branch. Spain, on the contrary, admits religion alone, and rejects

THE RACK, BY TORTURE, BY INQUISITION, BY IMPRISONMENT. Where they found reason to suspect any person, they might administer to him an oath, called *ex-officio*, by which he was bound to answer all questions; and *might thereby be obliged to accuse himself, or his most intimate friend. The fines which they levied were discretionary, and often occasioned the total ruin of the offender*, contrary to the established laws of the kingdom. *The imprisonment to which they condemned any delinquent was limited to no rule but their own pleasure. They assumed a power of imposing on the clergy what new articles of subscription, and consequently of faith, they thought proper.* * * * The more to enlarge their authority, they were empowered to punish all incest, adultery, fornication; all outrages, misbehaviors, and disorders in marriage. And *the punishments they might inflict were according to their wisdom, conscience, and discretion.* In a word, *this court was* A REAL INQUISITION, ATTENDED WITH ALL THE INIQUITIES, AS WELL AS CRUELTIES, INSEPARABLE FROM THAT TRIBUNAL." (1)

1578. "The 3d of February, early in the morning, John Nelson, for denying the queen's supremacy, and such other traitorous words against her majesty, was drawn from Tyburn, and there HANGED, BOWELLED, and QUARTERED." (2)

"The 7th of February, one named Sherwood was drawn from the Tower of London to Tyburn, and there HANGED, BOWELLED, and QUARTERED, for the like treason." (3)

1579. "Matthew Hamont, of Hetharset, three miles from Norwich, was convicted before the bishop of Norwich, *for that he denied Christ to be our Savior.* * * * * On the 20th of May, he was BURNED in the castle." (4)

1583 "On the 10th of January, at a sessions holden in the Justice Hall in the Old Bailey of London, for the jail delivery of Newgate, William Carter, of the city of London, was there indicted, arraigned, and condemned of HIGH TREASON, for *printing a seditious and traitorous book in English, entitled, 'A Treatise of Schisms,'* and was for the same, according to sentence pronounced against him, on the next morning, drawn from Newgate to Tyburn, and there HANGED, BOWELLED, and QUARTERED." (5)

"7th of February, were arraigned before Westminster, John Fen, George Haydock, John Murden, John Nutter, and Thomas Hemerford, all *five found guilty of high treason in being made priests beyond the seas, and by the pope's authority*, since a statute made, in *anno primo* of her majesty's reign, and had judgment to be HANGED,

---

(1) Hume's England, vol. iii. p. 126.
(2) Stowe's Chronicles, p. 684.
(3) Idem, p. 685.
(4) Stowe's Chronicles, p. 686.
(5) Idem, p. 698.

each Babel sect. How can two fundamental laws, diametrically opposite, be maintained by the same

---

BOWELLED, and QUARTERED; which were ALL EXECUTED at Tyburn, on the 12th of February." (1)

1583. "The 20th of February, Robert Southel, a Jesuit, was arraigned at the King's Bench bar, and the next day EXECUTED at Tyburn." (2)

"The 18th of February, Harrington, a seminary priest, was drawn from Newgate to Tyburn, and there *hanged*, CUT DOWN ALIVE, *struggled with the hangman*, but was BOWELLED and QUARTERED." (3)

1586. "Jan. 19, Nicholas Devorox was condemned for treason, in being made a seminary priest at Rheims, and for remaining here after the term of forty days from the session of the last parliament; also Edmond Barber, for being made a priest as aforesaid, and coming into this realm, was likewise condemned of treason; and both drawn to Tyburn, and there HANGED, BOWELLED, and QUARTERED, on the 21st of January." (4)

1586. "The 18th of April, in the Assizes holden in the Justice Hall, William Thompson, alias Blackbourne, made a priest at Rheims, and Richard Lea, alias Long, made a priest at Lyons, in France, and *remaining here contrary to the statute, were both condemned, and, on the 20th day of April*, drawn to Tyburn, and there HANGED, BOWELLED, and QUARTERED.' (5)

1586. "October 8, I. Law, 1. Adams, and Richard Dibdale, being before condemned for treason, in being made priests by order of the bishop of Rome, were drawn to Tyburn, and there HANGED, BOWELLED, and QUARTERED." (6)

1583. "The 23d of September, a seminary priest, named Flower, was HANGED, HEADED, and QUARTERED, at Kingston." (7)

"The 5th of October, John Wilden and William Hartley, made priests at Paris, and *remaining here contrary to a statute*, were HANGED, the one at Miles' End, and the other near the theatre; and Robert Sutton, for being reconciled to the see of Rome, was HANGED at Clerkenwell." (8)

"Christopher Bales, made priest beyond the sea, was convicted of TREASON, *for remaining in this realm, contrary to a statute;* also Nicholas Home and Alexander Blage, convicted of felony, ☞ for RELIEVING OF BALES, *contrary to the like statute;* these were ALL EXECUTED on the 4th of March: Bales was HANGED, BOWELLED, and QUARTERED, in Fleet Street, of Fetter Lane End; Home HANGED in Smithfield; and Blage HANGED at Gray's Inn Lane End." (9)

---

(1) Stowe's Chronicles, p. 698.
(2) Idem, p. 769.
(3) Idem, p. 766.
(4) Idem, p. 719.
(5) Idem, p. 720.
(6) Stowe's Chronicles, p. 741.
(7) Idem, p. 751.
(8) Idem, p. 751.
(9) Idem, p. 761.

means? The question is not to ascertain whether coercive laws should be made to insure to every

"10th of December, *three seminary priests, being in this realm contrary to the statute,* and ☞ FOUR OTHERS, FOR RELIEVING them, were executed; two of them, to wit, a seminary named Iremonger, and Swithen Wels, gentleman, in Gray's Inn Field; Blaston and White, seminaries, and three other abettors, at Tyburn. (1)
1588. Aug. 26. "At the sessions hall without Newgate, were condemned *six persons for having been made priests beyond the seas,* and remaining in this realm contrary to the statute, four temporal men for being reconciled to the Roman church, ☞ and FOUR OTHERS FOR RELIEVING AND ABETTING THE OTHERS!!! And, on the 28th, W. Dean and H. Wilby were HANGED at the Mile's End, W. Gunter at the theatre, R. Moorton and H. Moore, at Lincoln's Inn Fields, T. Astor at Clerkenwell, and James Clarkson between Branford and Hounslow; and, on the 30th of August, R. Hower, E. Shelley, R. Leigh, R. Martin, J. Roach, and MARGARET WARD, gentlewoman, (which Margaret Ward had conveyed a cord to a priest in Bridewell, whereby he let himself down and escaped,) *were hanged at Tyburn.*" (2)
1589. "Elias Thacker was HANGED at St. Edmondsbury, in Suffolk, on the 4th of June; and John Coping, on the 6th of the same month, for *spreading certain books,* seditiously penned by one Robert Browne, *against the Book of Common Prayer.*" (3)
Eodem anno. "September 17, John Lewis, *an obstinate heretic, denying the Godhead of Christ, and holding divers other detestable heresies,* was BURNED at Norwich." (4)
1589. "About this time, Francis Ket, pastor of art at Wymondham, was convicted before Edmond, bishop of Norwich, for holding divers detestable opinions against Christ our Savior, and was BURNED near the city of Norwich." (5)
"February 18, 1592, Thomas Pamorte was convicted of *two several high treasons,* the one *for being a seminary priest,* and remaining in this realm; and the other for *reconciling* John Barways, haberdasher, [to the Roman Catholic religion.] The said John Barways was likewise convicted of *high treason,* for being so reconciled, and also of ☞ *felony,* FOR RELIEVING THE SAID PRIEST, against the form of the statutes!!!!! On the 20th of February, Pamorte was executed at St. Paul's Churchyard." (6)
1596. July 12. "One Jones, alias Buckley, a priest made beyond the seas, having been arraigned at the King's Bench, and there condemned of treason, for coming into this realm, contrary to a statute, was drawn to St. Thomas's Waterings, and there HANGED, BOWELLED, and QUARTERED, *his head set upon the pillory at*

---

(1) Stowe's Chronicles, p. 764.
(2) Idem, p. 750.
(3) Idem, p. 697.
(4) Stowe's Chronicles, p. 697.
(5) Idem, p. 751.
(6) Idem, p. 764.

man *the liberty of doing what he likes*, for the solution of such a problem is easy enough; but the grand inquiry is, *how a nation can, within itself, without any such law, preserve unity of faith and worship.* The English in this respect adopt a sin-

---

Southwark, his quarters on the highways towards Newington Lambeth." (1)

1597. Feb. 27. "Mark Bakeworth and Thomas Filocks, seminary priests, were drawn to Tyburn, and there HANGED and QUARTERED, for coming into the realm contrary to the statute. ☞ Also, at the same time and same place, was *hanged a gentlewoman, called Mistress Ann Zane,* FOR RELIEVING A PRIEST, *contrary to the same statute!!!*" (2)

1600. "The 18th of February, John Pybush, a seminary priest, AFTER SEVEN YEARS' IMPRISONMENT in the King's Bench, was HANGED, BOWELLED, and QUARTERED, at St. Thomas's Waterings, *for coming into England contrary to the statute, anno 27 of the queen.*" (3)

1602. "The 18th of April, Peter Bulloche, stationer, and one named Docker, *for printing of books offensive,* were HANGED at Tyburn." (4)

"The 20th of April, Stickbourne, William Kenion, and James Page, *seminary priests,* were drawn to Tyburn, and there HANGED, BOWELLED, and QUARTERED, *for coming into this realm contrary to the statute* anno 27." (5)

"The 17th of February, William Anderson, a seminary priest, was drawn to Tyburn, and there HANGED, BOWELLED, and QUARTERED, *for being found in England, contrary to the statute* anno 27." (6)

1600. "The 21st of June, John Rigby was drawn from the King's Bench in Southwark to St. Thomas's Waterings, and there HANGED, BOWELLED, and QUARTERED, *for being reconciled contrary to the statute.*" (7)

"Also, in the month of July, were DRAWN, HANGED, and QUARTERED, at Lincoln, two priests, named Hunt, and Sprat, for coming into the realm contrary to the statute; two other priests, Edward King and Robert Nuttar, *were likewise* EXECUTED for the like offence, at Lancaster; also Thomas Palafar, a priest, EXECUTED at Durham, and ☞ *a gentleman with him, for* RECEIVING and LODGING HIM IN HIS HOUSE!!!!!!" (8)

---

(1) Stowe's Chronicles, p. 787.
(2) Idem, p. 794.
(3) Idem, p. 787.
(4) Idem, p. 804.
(5) Stowe's Chronicles, p. 804.
(6) Idem, p. 812.
(7) Idem, p. 790.
(8) Idem, p. 790.

gular mode of reasoning; under the specious name of *toleration*, they establish an absolute indifference for religion in point of fact; they then, according to *their rule*, pass sentence upon such nations as view this indifference as the most pregnant source of misery and crime!

We are thus happy, say they: grant it, if the unity of religion and an awful futurity are not viewed by them in a proper light; but, arguing from these two contrary propositions, how can their statesmen accomplish the primary intention of all legislation?

God has spoken: it is our duty to believe. The religion he established is ONE, as HE is ONE. *Truth* is in its very nature *intolerant;* to profess, therefore, a religious toleration, is to profess doubt, or, in other words, to exclude faith. Woe, a thousand woes, to the stupid imprudence that accuses us of *damning men!* It is God who damns; it is He who has sent his deputies, — "*Go and teach all nations; and, lo! I am with you all days, even to the consummation of the world.*" "*If he will not hear the church, let him be to thee as the heathen and the publican.*" "*He that believes shall be saved; he who believes not shall be condemned.*"

Sensible as we are of his loving-kindness, can we forget any of his divine oracles, or precepts? Although he *cannot tolerate* error, we know that, under certain circumstances, he *can pardon* it. We shall never cease to implore his forgiveness of it; but then we shall never cease to place all our hopes in him in behalf of unintentional error; and shall ever fear and tremble, when we recollect that God alone knows it.

Such is the profession of a Spaniard's faith, and of millions besides. It necessarily supposes in its adepts an ardent *proselytism*, an uncompromising aversion to every thing in the shape of innovation or change, an ever-watchful eye upon the schemes and machinations of impiety, a voice of thunder and an uplifted, indefatigable arm against it. In nations where this doctrine is professed, Legislation keeps her eyes in a special manner upon a future state, believing *that every thing else is added to them;* whereas other nations, that have not *the fear of the Lord, which is the beginning of wisdom,* before them, carelessly and suicidally act upon the principle of Tacitus, (Annals, book 73,) "DEORUM INJURIÆ DIIS CURA," (*Insults to the gods are their own concern.*) Futurity to such nations is a very nothing. The common average of man's life, which may be considered as fixed at twenty-five years, or, according to Scripture, at threescore and ten, concentrates all the attention, and constitutes the only subject of *their* legislation. Improvements in science and the arts, in agriculture, commerce, and manufactures, occupy all their time.

They dare not publicly assert that *they feel no interest in religion;* their very actions, however, suppose it; and all their legislative enactments may be correctly set down for tacit proofs of *materialism*, inasmuch as there is no provision made for the soul, or eternity. There cannot, therefore, be any point of contract, or similarity, between these two systems. A new-fangled system, which is identified with an indifference for, if not a total aversion from, an aged and useful institution, should not censure it, until it had pointed out an infallible means of self-defence, without having recourse to vigilance and salutary rigor — a consummation devoutly to be wished, but which as yet has never been realized.

But what proofs of Christian patience and meekness had England given, when she so loudly preached up the doctrine of *toleration* to other nations, and when she fancied that *her own* religion was attacked? Infidel Hume, the pensioned libeller of Catholicity, and who sacrificed truth, wherever the religion of Christ was concerned, on the idolatrous altar of the golden calf, upbraids England for practising *her inquisitorial* cruelty upon the Catholics, whose only crime was their allegiance to the constitution, and to the church which Jesus God established upon earth! He acknowledges that "*the whole tyranny of the Inquisition, though without its order, was introduced into the kingdom.*" This individual, in his anti-Catholic malice, attacks this civil tribunal of Spain! Ought he not to have information to know, and honesty to confess, that such a tribunal, supported, as it is, by *mercy* on the one side, and *justice* on the other, must be only *salutarily* severe, and *not*

cruel? Whereas, a tribunal that condemns without legal form, is, to all intents and purposes, an *assassin*, and, of course, execrable in the extreme. In the reign of the ferocious Elizabeth, "*whoever in any way reconciled any one to the Church of Rome, or was himself reconciled, was declared guilty of high treason!!!*"

Any person, over sixteen years of age, who refused, for more than a month, to frequent the Protestant service, was put in prison. If he continued obstinate, he was forever banished from the kingdom; and if, unfortunately, he had returned to see his family, or relieve his parents, he was executed as a traitor!*

CAMPIAN, renowned for science, eloquence, and purity of morals, was martyred in her infernal reign, merely as a missioner, and a comforter of his brethren! *Accused* by a gang of profligates of *having entered into a plot against the queen,* † he was *racked* to such a degree of inhumanity, that the jailer, who was an eye-witness to the scene, observed, "*This poor man will be soon stretched a half foot longer.*" Three of his judges, horrified at this brutal injustice, retired, and refused to participate in his *judiciary* murder. ‡

---

* Nat. Alex. Hist. Eccles. Sacc. xvi. cap. 5, 169. Chaloner's Memoirs, &c. London. Der Triumph der Philosophie, 8vo. vol. i. p. 448.

† How *faithfully* her brother-monster Robespierre imitated her, upon the plea of securing himself and his faction in power!

‡ Edmund Campian, born in London, anno 1540, and educated in *Christ Church* School, or hospital of *blue-coats*, preëminently distinguished himself for his classical literature. He was selected to de-

WALPOLE was likewise condemned and executed! The queen offered him pardon on the scaffold, if he

liver a Latin oration before Queen Mary, upon her accession to the throne, in 1553. He entered Oxford University and obtained the degree of *master of arts* in 1564. About the same time, says WOOD, "He took holy orders according to the *Church of England*, from the hands of *Richard Cheney*, bishop of *Gloucester*, who had encouraged him in his studies.—*Athen Oxon.* p. 206." When Elizabeth visited that university, in 1566, he pronounced a Latin oration before her also, and "was respondent at the public act held in her presence; on which occasion he acquitted himself to the great satisfaction both of the queen and of all the university. *He had, for some time, been very uneasy within himself, concerning the principles and tenets of the Church of England; and the scruple growing upon him in the year 1568, when he was one of the proctors of the university, the year following he forsook that communion, notwithstanding the fair prospect he had of advancing himself.*" He retired to Ireland, and, during his abode there, had frequent conversations with several persons of distinction, who, being great admirers of his parts and learning, seemed to be influenced by him in matters of religion. This being observed by some *zealots of the reformation*, he was obliged to return privately into England. He next visited the continent, became a Jesuit, and, owing to the frightful desolation which Protestantism, by the murder of the Catholic clergy and laity, and by the robbery and burning of churches, had caused in his once happy, native land, he, in compliance with the order of his superior, revisited England as a missioner. "Soon after, he was seized in the house of *Edward Yates, Esq.*, of *Lyford*, in *Berkshire*, where he and some other missionaries were assembled upon the duties of their function. He was carried in triumph through *Abingdon*, *Henley*, and *Colebrook*, with a paper fixed on his hat, signifying his name, character, and the pretended crimes he was charged with, and committed close prisoner in the Tower. Here he underwent a general persecution from the tongues and hands of his enemies. He suffered in his person no less than in his reputation, BEING SEVERAL TIMES PUT TO THE RACK to extort a confession of, I don't know what contrivances were carrying on abroad against the queen and government!" To such extremes of cruelty will dastard, ill-got, guilty power resort to secure its iniquitous ascendency. He was *of course* CONDEMNED TO DIE at Tyburn, December 1, 1581. CAMBDEN says that this execution was a stroke of policy to *pacify* the nation, which, at that time, was in a great ferment, on account of the duke of Anjou, who was then in London, paying his addresses to the *meek and virtuous virgin* Elizabeth. The Protestants apprehended that, in the case of this marriage, an end would come to *their religion*. "Therefore," continues Cambden, [Vide Annals Queen Eliz. p. 130,] "during his stay here, to take away all fear which possessed men's minds that religion would be altered and Popery tolerated, *being overcome by importunate entreaties*, she permitted that Edmund Campian aforesaid, of the Society

would acknowledge her *spiritual supremacy!* He of course refused, and was sacrificed.

Who, that is acquainted with history, is ignorant of the horrible cruelties committed in her reign against the CATHOLICS of IRELAND?* Who has

---

of *Jesus, Ralph Sherwin, Luke Kimby,* and *Alexander Briant,* PRIESTS, should be arraigned, &c. &c.; and THIS HAS EVER SINCE BEEN THE METHOD OF THE MINISTRY IN REGARD OF CATHOLICS. NO SOONER WAS THERE ANY PROSPECT OF THEIR INTEREST INCREASING, BUT POLITICIANS WERE AT WORK TO FIX SOME DAMNABLE CONTRIVANCE UPON THEM, IN ORDER TO RENDER THEM ODIOUS AND PUT A STOP TO WHAT THEY CALLED THE GROWTH OF POPERY!!!" And *such* is the fiendish plan adopted by heretics, even at the present day, against the Catholic Church and its members. How striking the parallel between such a course of conduct and that adopted by the Pharisees of old against the adorable Savior of the world! The accusers of the enlightened, upright, and martyred Campian, were a wretch named *George Eliot,* another called *Slade, an apostate,* and formerly a *servant* in the English College at Rome, *Anthony Mundy,* a profligate *player, Cradock,* and *Norton,* who, in their rambles abroad, had been *entertained* and *relieved* in said college! O *Reformation,* foul and false! to what monsters hast thou given birth! — *Translator.*

* "All Popish archbishops, bishops, vicars-general, deans, Jesuits, monks, friars, and *all other regular Popish clergy,* and all Papists exercising any ecclesiastical jurisdiction, shall depart this kingdom before the 1st of May, 1698. And if any of them shall be, at any time after the said day, within this kingdom, *they shall be imprisoned, and remain there without bail till they be transported* beyond the seas, out of the king's dominions, wherever the king, his heirs, or successors, or chief governors of this kingdom, shall think fit; and *if any so transported shall return again into this kingdom, then to be guilty of high treason, and to suffer accordingly!!!"* (1)

"Every Popish priest, who is now in this kingdom, shall, at the next quarter sessions, to be held in the several counties, or counties of cities or towns, next after the feast of St. John Baptist, 1704, return his name and place of abode, together with his age, the parish of which he pretends to be Popish priest, the time and place of his receiving Popish orders, and from whom; and shall then enter into recognizance, with two sufficient sureties, each of the penalty of fifty pounds, to be of peaceable behavior, and *not remove out of such county* where his abode is into any other part of this kingdom." (2)

"No Popish priest shall exercise the function or office of a Popish priest but in the parish where the said Popish priest did officiate at the time of registering the Popish clergy, and for which parish also

---

(1) Robins's Abridgment of the Irish Statutes, p. 451.
(2) Idem, p. 458.

not heard of the cruelties of *Lord*, or rather *monster*,

---

he was registered, and in no other parish whatsoever, *under the penalties as any Popish regular convict is liable unto.*" (1) What an atrocious system for the extermination of Catholicity!

"Every person whatsoever, exercising the office or function of a Popish priest, found in this kingdom after the 24th of June, 1705, other than such as are registered pursuant to the above act, *shall be liable to such penalties, forfeitures, and punishments, as are imposed upon Popish archbishops, bishops, &c.*" (2)

"Every Popish clergyman coming into this kingdom after the 1st of January, 1703, shall be liable to such penalties, forfeitures, and punishments, as are imposed on Popish archbishops, bishops, &c." (3)

"Every Popish parish priest, that shall keep any Popish curate, assistant, or coadjutor, shall lose the benefit of having been registered, *and shall incur all the penalties of a Popish regular, and shall be prosecuted as such;* and every such Popish curate, assistant, or coadjutor, *shall be deemed as a Popish regular, and shall be prosecuted as such.*" (4)

"If any Popish priest, or reputed Popish priest, or any person pretending to be a Popish priest, or any degraded clergyman, or any layman pretending to be a clergyman of the Church of Ireland, as by law established, shall, after the 25th day of April, 1726, *celebrate any marriage between two Protestants, or reputed Protestants, or between a Protestant, or reputed Protestant, and a Papist,* such Popish priest, &c., *shall be guilty of felony, and shall suffer death as a felon, without benefit of clergy or of the statute!!!!*" (5)

"No Papist, after the 20th of January, 1695, shall be capable to have, or keep in his possession, or in the possession of any other, to his use, or at his disposition, *any horse, gelding, or mare, of the value of 5l. or more;* and if any person of the Protestant religion shall make discovery thereof, upon oath, to any two justices of the peace, or to the chief magistrate of any city or town corporate, they may, within their respective limits, by warrant under their hands and seals, authorize such person, in the daytime only, to search for and secure all such horses; *and, in case of resistance, to break open any door, and bring such horse or horses before them;* and such discoverer, (being of the Protestant religion,) paying, or making tender, before such justices, mayor, &c., of the sum of 5l. 5s. to the owner or possessor of such horse, after such payment, or tender and refusal, the property of such horse or horses shall *be vested in the person making such discovery and tender,* as if the same had been bought and sold in market overt!!!" (6)

"*All settlements, fines, common recoveries, and other conveyances, had or made* since the 1st of January, 1703, of any lands, &c., by any Papist, or by any Protestant who turned Papist, since the said

---

(1) Robins's Abridgment of the Irish Statutes, p. 464.
(2) Idem, p. 459.   (5) Idem, p. 388.
(3) Idem, p. 453.   (6) Idem, p. 450.
(4) Idem, p. 462.

1st of January, 1703, or by any such Papist with his then Protestant wife, who hath turned Papist as aforesaid, whereby any Protestant is barred of any estate, in reversion, or remainder, whereunto such Protestant was intituled at the time of levying such fine, suffering such recovery, or making such conveyance, *shall, as to such Protestant, be null and void.*" (1)

"All collateral and other securities, by mortgages, judgments, statutes merchant, or of the staple, or otherwise, *which have been, or hereafter shall be, made, or entered into,* to cover, support, or secure and make good any bargain, sale, confirmation, release, feoffment, lease, or other conveyance, contrary to 2 Anne, ses. 1, c. 6, are void to the purchaser of any the said lands or tenements in trust for, or for the benefit of, any Papist, as likewise to any such Papist, his heirs and assigns; and all such lands, &c., so conveyed or leased, or to be conveyed or leased, to any Papist, or to the use of, or in trust for, any Papist, contrary to the said act, and all such collateral securities as are, or shall be, made, or entered into, to cover, support, secure, or make good, the same, *may be sued for by any Protestant,* by his proper action, real, personal, or mixed, founded on this act, in any of her majesty's courts of law or equity, if the nature of the case shall require it!!!!"

"Provided any Protestant may prefer one or more bill or bills in the chancery, or chancery of exchequer, against any person concerned in such sale, lease, mortgage, or encumbrance, and against all persons privy to such trust for Papists; and to compel such person to discover such trusts, and answer all matters relating thereunto, as by such bill shall be required; to which bill, no plea or demurrer shall be allowed; *but the defendant shall answer the same on oath at large, which answer shall be good evidence against the defendant* in actions brought upon this act; and that all issues, in any suit founded on this act, *shall be tried by none but known Protestants!!!!*" (2)

"None shall, from the said 29th of December, bury any dead in any suppressed monastery, abbey, or convent, that is not made use of for celebrating divine service according to the liturgy of the Church of Ireland by the law established, or within the precincts thereof, *upon pain of ten pounds.*" (3)

"From the first of Michaelmas Term, 1708, no Papist shall serve, or be returned to serve, on any grand jury in the Queen's Bench, or before justices of Assizes, Oyer and Terminer, or Jail Delivery, or Quarter Sessions, unless it appear to the court that a sufficient number of Protestants cannot then be had for the service; and in all trials of issues, on any presentment, indictment, or information, or action on statute, for any offence committed by Papists, in breach of such laws, *the plaintiff or prosecutor may challenge any Papist returned as juror, and assign as a cause that he is a Papist, which challenge shall be allowed of!!!!*" (4)

"No Papist shall be guardian unto, or have the tuition or custody of, any orphan or child under the age of twenty-one years; but the

---

(1) Robins's Abridgment of the Irish Statutes, p. 460.
(2) Idem, pp. 464, 465.
(3) Idem, p. 452.
(4) Idem, p. 459.

same (where the person intituled to, or having the guardianship of, such child, is or shall be a Papist) shall be disposed of by chancery, to some near relation of such orphan, &c., being a Protestant, to whom the estate cannot descend!!

"If any Papist shall take upon him the guardianship or tuition of any orphan or child contrary to this act, *he shall forfeit* 500*l.*, *to be recovered by action of debt!!*" (1)

"The lieutenants, &c., or the major part of them, may cause to be raised upon the Popish inhabitants, and upon every person who shall refuse to take the oath of abjuration, (which oath any justice of the peace may administer,) *double the sum they should have paid by virtue of this act*, in case they had been Protestants!!" (2)

"In case such Papist shall neglect or refuse to find such sufficient man, *he shall forfeit double the sum as a Protestant should forfeit*, in case such Protestant should neglect to attend the service of the militia, when thereunto required, by beat of drum, or sound of trumpet, as aforesaid." (3)

"Leases of the premises to be made to Protestants only, at the full improved rent, without any fine. *Leases to, or in trust for, Papists, or assigned to them, to be void*, and the lessor, assignor, and lessee, or assignee, accepting or occupying such lands, *to forfeit treble the yearly value!!*" (4)

"Every Papist, after the time aforesaid, shall be disabled to purchase, either in his own name, or in the name of any other, to his use, or in trust for him, any manors, lands, hereditaments, or any rents or profits out of the same, or any leases, or terms thereof, other than for a term of years not exceeding thirty-one years, whereon a rent, *not less than two thirds of the improved yearly value*, at the time of making such lease, shall be reserved and made payable during such term!!" (5)

"After the 1st of May, 1746, every marriage celebrated by a Popish priest, between a Papist and any person who hath been, or hath professed himself or herself to be, a Protestant, at any time within twelve months of such celebration of marriage, or between two Protestants, *shall be null and void to all intents and purposes, without any process, judgment, or sentence of the law, whatsoever.*" (6)

"All Papists within this kingdom of Ireland, before the 1st of March next, shall discover and deliver up to some justice of the peace, *all their arms, armor, and ammunition, of what kind soever, in their possession;* and, after that time, any two or more justices of the peace, within their respective limits, and all mayors, sheriffs, and chief officers of cities, &c., in their liberties, by themselves, or their warrants, under their hands and seals, may search for, seize, or cause to be searched for and seized, and take into their custody, all such arms, &c., as shall be concealed in any house, lodging, or other places where they suspect any such to be." (7)

---

(1) Robins's Abridgment of the Irish Statutes, p. 454.
(2) Idem, p. 407.
(3) Idem, p. 409.
(4) Idem, p. 26.
(5) Idem, p. 454
(6) 2 Geo. II. xiii. 19.
(7) Robins, p. 448.

Fitz-William?* *Elizabeth was well acquainted with all this.* At the present day, a manuscript

"Two justices of peace, or the magistrate of any corporation, are empowered to summon before them any persons whatsoever, to tender them an oath, by which they oblige them to discover all persons who have any arms concealed, contrary to law. Their refusal, or declining to appear, or, on appearing, their refusal to inform, subjects them to the severest penalties. *If peers or peeresses are summoned* (for they may be summoned by the bailiff of a corporation of six cottages) *to perform this honorable service, and they refuse to inform, the first offence is* 300*l. penalty; the second, premunire, that is to say, imprisonment for life, and forfeiture of all their goods.* Persons of an inferior order are for the first offence fined 30*l.*; for the second, they, too, are subjected to premunire." (1)

"If any mayor, justice of peace, or other officer, shall neglect, knowingly and voluntarily, to do his duty in execution of this act, he shall, for every such neglect, forfeit 50*l.*, to be recovered by action of debt, &c., one moiety to her majesty, &c., the other to him that will sue for the same." (2)

"*If any Papist shall publicly teach school, or instruct youth in learning in any private house, or shall be entertained to instruct youth, as usher or assistant to any Protestant schoolmaster, he shall be esteemed a Popish regular clergyman, and prosecuted as such, and shall incur such penalties and forfeitures as any Popish regular convict is liable unto.*" (3) What an infernal law in this Pandemoniac code! What heretical tongue can have the impiety to declare that the *Roman Catholic religion* perpetuates ignorance! Blasphemous assertion! Has not the ungodly *Reformation* legalized impiety and murder, rapine, bodily and mental slavery, and all the abominations of her partner — Antichrist?

"Any person that shall, from the 1st of May, knowingly conceal or entertain any such archbishop, bishops, &c., hereby required to depart out of this kingdom, or that, after the said day, shall come into this kingdom, shall, for the first offence, *forfeit twenty pounds;* for the second, *double that sum;* and if he offend the third time, *shall forfeit all his lands and tenements of freehold, or inheritance during his life; and also his goods and chattels!!!!*" (4)

"The eldest son, conforming, immediately acquires, *in the lifetime of his father*, the permanent part, what our law calls *the reversion and inheritance of the estate;* and he discharges it by retrospect, and annuls every sort of voluntary settlement made by the father ever so long before his conversion! This he may sell or dispose of immediately, and alienate it from the family forever!!!" (5)

* They cannot be excused upon any principle of justice or necessity. — *Edinb. Review*, Oct. No. 9, p. 156.

(1) Burke, v. p. 195.
(2) Robins, p. 459.
(3) Idem, p. 612.
(4) Robins, p. 452.
(5) Burke, v. p. 187.

letter can be seen in the archives of Trinity College, Dublin, wherein an *officer* named LEC describes these damning cruelties. "*They are such,*" says he, "*that we should rather expect to find them in the history of a Turkish province, than in that of an English province.*"* "And yet," adds the learned Cambden, "*Elizabeth did not believe that the greatest part of those unfortunate priests, thus butchered by the tribunals, were guilty of any crime against the country.*"† *Amiable* woman! In a word, a digest of the *laws*, (if the term can be thus profaned,) which were passed against Catholics, and especially against CATHOLIC IRELAND, would form a code of oppression unexampled in the annals of the universe, for robbery, atrocity, perfidy, slaughter, blasphemy, and crime.‡

BACON, in what he called his *Natural History*, speaks with perhaps more than becoming gravity of a certain magic ointment: among other ingredients of the singular compound, he mentions *the fat of a boar and of a bear, killed during the venereal orgasm;* and, moreover, *the exudation which is collected from the skull of an unburied human body.* He states that it might be hard to procure the two former; but, as to the last mentioned, he dispassionately observes,

---

* Edinb. Review, Oct. No. 9, p. 159.
† Cambden, Annal. Eng. edit. 1615, vol. i. p. 137.
‡ *I think I can hardly overrate the malignity of the principles of the Protestant ascendency, as they affect Ireland. No country, I believe, since the world began, suffered so much on account of religion.* — Burke, vol. v. pp. 232, 233.

"*It could be certainly found in great abundance, in Ireland, upon the human carcasses which are thrown in heaps into the — sewers*"!!!*

I request, sir, that you will recollect that, in the country which bears witness to such inexorable persecution, it is *notorious*, and even acknowledged in parliament, as a natural consequence of the same unslumbering, tyrannic spirit, that, were the king of England to embrace any other religion than the Protestant, as established by act of parliament, he would forfeit his crown!!!† I believe, in my con-

---

* *Sylva Sylvarum*, or a Natural History, cent. x. No. 998.

† See Cobbett's Parliamentary Debates, vol. iv. London, in 8vo. col. 677, 721.

ROYAL CORONATION OATH. — See *Magna Charta*, printed by Richard Tottel, Anno 1556, fol. 164 and 166, for several oaths there appointed to be taken.

By 1 Gulielm. et Mar. sess. I. c. 6, *En.*, the following oath is to be administered to every king and queen, at the time of their coronation, viz. : —

The *Archbishop* or *Bishop* shall say, — "Will you solemnly promise and swear, to govern the people of this kingdom of England, and the dominions thereunto belonging, according to the statutes in parliament agreed on, and the laws and customs of the same?"

The *King* and *Queen* shall say, — "I solemnly promise so to do."

Archbishop or *Bishop*. — "Will you, to the utmost of your power, cause law and justice, in mercy, to be executed in all your judgments?"

King and *Queen*. — "I will."

Archbishop or *Bishop*. — "Will you, to the utmost of your power, maintain the laws of God, the true profession of the gospel, and the *Protestant reformed religion, established by law?* And will you preserve to the bishops and clergy of this realm, and to the churches committed to their charge, all such rights and privileges as by law do or shall appertain to them, or any of them?"

King and *Queen*. — "All this I promise to do."

After this, the *King* and *Queen*, laying his and her hand upon the Holy Gospels, shall say, — "The things which I have here before promised I will perform and keep : — So help me God!"

Then the king and queen shall kiss the book.

Extracted from pages 425, 426, of Robins's "Abridgment." — *Translator*.

science, that Englishmen would think twice before they would attempt to enforce this law; but even supposing it, I consider it as strange, indeed, that an *English parliament* should have the incontestable right of dethroning an intelligent, a virtuous and great king, for having become a *Catholic,* and that a *Catholic king* should not have a right to punish an immoral, a profligate *subject* who turned *Protestant.* How inconsistent can nations become! nay, how very ridiculous do they unconsciously prove themselves so to the world! An Englishman would satisfactorily make it appear that his king has no right or control over the conscience of an Englishman, and that, if he presumed to restore the primitive faith, the nation would have the right of making his *sacred person* responsible for it; but ask this same individual, *" How, then, had Henry VIII. and Elizabeth more right over the conscience of the people, in their iniquitous reigns, than even George IV. at the present day? How were the English, at that epoch, culpable in resisting those two sovereigns, who were, to all intents and purposes, tyrants in regard to them, according to the English theory?"* He would unhesitatingly exclaim, *" O! that is a quite different case!"* We would take him at his word, and say that there is a difference indeed; for the patriotic and religious people of England, who opposed the tyrannic and murderous heresy of Henry and his spurious daughter Elizabeth, justly grounded their resistance upon their possession of a holy, an untransferable right of sixteen centuries, while the profligate impugners of this right usurped a power engendered by blasphemy and lust, and which was destitute of morality, virtue, religion, or time to support or sanctify it. God forbid that I should in any way revive the dismal horrors of the *mock* reformation. Nothing is more abhorrent to my feelings; but duty obliges me to be thus far particular to prove that England and her descendants ought to be the very last in the world to harp on so sensitive a chord, and to censure Spain for her civil or religious legislation. Although England had more ample means of self-defence than any other nation of Europe, she became a prey to the most revolting and horrid excesses. When she banished a lawful king, and beheaded another, when she was frightfully convulsed by the demoniac spirit of *Puritanism*, and repeatedly tortured by a self-inflicted rebellion, and was finally calmed down by a remedy of a *somewhat* dubious nature, it must be evident, to every sensible, virtuous mind, that it badly becomes her to run down Spain for *her* "*detestable Inquisition;*" as if the world were not convinced that Spain *alone*, by this institution *alone*, displayed her wisdom to such a degree as to elicit the admiration even of a Voltaire, by keeping at bay the legion monster of heresy and infidelity, revolution, carnage, and crime! The miserable Voltaire once observed that "He who lives in a house of glass should not throw stones at his neighbor." How badly did he apply the maxim!

Has the British government ever done otherwise? But perhaps it may be said that "*the convulsions of England are at an end; and, although its present state cost it torrents of blood, yet she is now on so enviable a point of elevation as to excite the wonder of all the nations of the earth.*"

In answer to this remark, I shall say that no one is obliged to purchase a future and uncertain benefit by great and positive misfortunes. The sovereign who would calculate thus, is far from being acquainted with wisdom or virtue. Consequently, the kings of Spain, who, by shedding a comparatively insignificant portion of blood at *once rebellious and impure*, saved an ocean of the pure, patriotic, and Christian blood of the land, had formed a much better estimate, and are relatively innocent. Besides, it has cost England not only torrents of blood to attain this truly unenviable elevation, but even her very faith, her very all; as, *without it, it is impossible to please God.* Her persecution apparently ceased with her *established* faith: no wonder, then, that she should be proud! In the present age, mankind, it would seem, cautiously set out with a system of materalism, and by far too large a number of those who are called intelligent are, in the long run, unconsciously carried away by its influence. If this world be the SUMMUM BONUM, and eternity be only a dream, the reasoning and conduct of England are correct; *but, if all here below is vanity and vexation of spirit,* and "heaven itself points out *an hereafter,* and intimates *eternity* to man," then, indeed, has worldly-mindedness reason to tremble, and adopt a different plan of conduct. England will unhesitatingly reply to her sister nation, "*Spain! you have lost your faith, and I am of the right creed.*" As it requires not the wisdom of a philosopher to expect such an objection, neither does it that of a theologian to answer it thus: "*Prove to us, then, that you believe in your religion, and let us see how you defend it.*" There is no well-informed man who does not know the propriety of adhering, on such an occasion, to these two points; for, in reality, all the boasted *toleration* of England is nothing more nor less than a total indifference for genuine religion. The true believer must necessarily be charitable; yet his toleration must have bounds. If England tolerates religion and its various sects, it is because she has no more faith than appears in her Thirty-nine Articles. If England had a fixed form of faith, she would think more favorably of the numerous Christian creeds, in proportion as they approximated to her own. Such, however, is not the case, and she would a thousand times prefer to see a Socinian, Turk, Jew, or atheist, in her House of Commons, than a Roman Catholic, however intelligent and virtuous! Is not such a *fact* as this sufficient proof that the Christian faith is not an object of her solicitude and esteem? Whereas, then, she has visibly and entirely lost her faith, respectable as she is in other respects, she has lost the right of commenting upon or censuring a nation who considers the loss of her faith as the greatest of all human calamities, and who adopts the most efficient and salutary means to prevent it.

The more closely you examine this subject, the more convinced you will be that what is generally called religion, in many countries, is a mere hatred of a regular and exclusive system. Such a *mania* is termed Protestantism, or nicknamed piety, zeal, faith, reformation, and orthodoxy.* An English bishop lately asserted — not in a work of erudition, or polem-

---

* One of the greatest statesmen of the age, (although he exercised his talents on a narrow stage,) and a Protestant by birth, once observed to me, " *Had it not been for you we could not exist.*" This remark was as profound as correct. He well knew that the religion of every *Protestant,* or *negative* character, consists of a common hatred of, or an aversion to, that which is of a *firm* and *affirmative* nature. Remove the object of this hatred or aversion, and what then remains? Nothing.

Well may it be said that the Catholic religion is of a *firm and affirmative* nature. "Thou art Peter," [he was not a Protestant *reformer;* he was, on the contrary, one of those who drew the constitution of the Christian faith in which we find this valuable clause, " *I believe in the Holy Catholic Church,*"] " and upon this *rock* I will *build* my Church, and the gates of hell *shall not prevail* against it." "Lo, I am with you all days, even to the consummation of the world." Did he ever make such a promise to Luther, Calvin, Henry VIII., Queen Elizabeth, or the more modern authors and framers of creeds, and *curious* modes of worship? "The Church is the pillar and ground of truth. And I will ask the Father, and he *shall* give you another Paraclete, (the Spirit of truth,) that he may abide with you *forever.* And they were all filled with the Holy Ghost, and they began to speak with divers tongues, according as the Holy Ghost gave them to speak." Where was the *necessity* of *protesting* against such a Church, thus founded and confirmed by the sanctifying influence and perpetual protection and presence of the Savior and the Holy Ghost? Does man sin against the Holy Ghost when he wantonly despises and calumniates the Church with which He and the adorable Redeemer abide forever? Does not the Savior say that " whoever sins against the Holy Ghost, it shall not be forgiven him in this life, nor in the next "? Ask St. Matthew.— *Translator.*

ical theology, but in a pastoral charge to his subjects — the following paradox, that the *English Church is not Protestant!* This, to be sure, is rather curious. I would respectfully ask the right reverend gentleman, "What, then, is it?" He vouchsafes to answer, "It is SCRIPTURAL!"* He undoubtedly means that the Church of England *is not* Protestant, but that *it is* a Protestant Church, because *Protestantism* essentially consists in its *scripturality;* that is, it considers the *Scripture* to be the sole guide and rule of faith, the only proper authority! You cannot but remember, sir, that, in the month of March, 1805, an English bishop was consulted by a lady upon an important and very difficult question, namely, *whether she could give her daughter in marriage to a certain gentleman who was neither a Catholic nor Protestant.* The parties concerned acquainted me with the bishop's answer: you recollect that you were present on the occasion, and it appeared to me the most curious circumstance I ever read of or heard. The sapient prelate at first explained the great distinction between the fundamental and non-fundamental articles. He stated that all men who agreed upon the former were *Christians.* "*Besides,*" said he,

---

* "Our articles and liturgy do not exactly correspond with the sentiments of any of the eminent reformers upon the continent, nor with the creeds of any of the Protestant churches which are there established;" [as if a church could not *protest* because it did not *protest* with others!] " Our church is not Lutheran; it is not Calvinist; it is not Arminian: it is SCRIPTURAL." — *A Charge delivered to the Clergy of the Diocese of Lincoln,* &c. London, Cadel & Davis, 1803, 4to. — Such is the palliative slang from the Genesis to the Apocalypse of all the *reformationites.*

"*every one has a conscience, and God will judge us.*" He himself knew a gentleman, educated at Eton and Cambridge, who, having duly examined the grounds of the two religions to the best of his power, determined in favor of the Church of Rome. He did not blame him, and consequently believed that this scrupulous and affectionate mother could, with a safe conscience, give her daughter in marriage to a gentleman who was not of the English Church, even although the children of this marriage were brought up in the religion of the father. "*If,*" continues the bishop, "*in every other respect, the match meets with her approbation and that of her parents, it must not be declined from any apprehension of her children's salvation being risked by being educated in the Roman Church, especially as, when they arrive at mature age, they will be at liberty to judge for themselves which, of all the Christian churches, is most suitable to the gospel of Christ.*"

This decision of a Protestant bishop might excite horror in the bosom of many of the *reformation* family, while, at the same time, it does honor to his head and heart. Even had he not been entitled to it on several other occasions, and enjoyed an extensive and well-merited reputation, this, of itself, would be sufficient to secure him the profound esteem of every respectable man in society. He certainly must have possessed much moral independence, a tender conscience, and an extraordinary degree of courage, in thus frankly acknowledging the presumed equality of all the religious systems, or, in other words, the *nullity of his own*. Such, in reality, is the faith of the bishops of a famous nation, that may be justly considered the very head of the Protestant system. One of its advocates publicly blushed at its origin, and would, if possible, obliterate from its forehead *the mark* which constituted the essence of that church. Its very existence was identified with a *protest* against aged, venerable, and holy authority: no difference, therefore, in the mode of *protesting* could in any way alter its essence; for, when it ceased to *protest*, it would have ceased to *exist*. Another of that mitred body goes upon the principle of private judgment, which is the very soul of the Protestant system, and, with a frankness worthy of a better cause, comes to the following inevitable conclusion: " Man having over his fellow-man no other power than what philosophy can give him, it necessarily follows, with the exception of the sciences, that there is no universal, and especially no divine, truth. Any appeal to a book would be not only an error, but downright nonsense, since the point at issue is the book itself. If I believed, with a divine faith, the tenets which I teach by the authority of the king, I should be evidently wrong in advising to have unfortunate children brought up in error, and reserving for them the privilege of returning to the truth until they had arrived at maturity, and were capable of judging for themselves; but I do not believe in these tenets; at least my belief in them is of a *human* nature, equal, for instance, to my belief in the system of Stahl, which, of course, will not prevent another from believing in that of Lavoisier; and, therefore, I see no reason why a chemist of either school should refuse his daughter to a member of the other."

Such is the exact meaning of the Protestant bishop's answer, which may be regarded as so much wisdom and honesty combined; but I would again ask him, " What can be the *faith* of a country where the chief pastors think and reason thus? What influence can *they* have over the great mass of the people?" I have known many Protestants, and particularly those of the English school, from whom I have learned the nature of Protestantism. In them I never saw but deists, more or less qualified by their Bible, and altogether strangers to what we call *divine* or *revealed faith*. The very opinion they have of the ministers of their religion is an infallible sign of the doctrine which their preachers taught them, for between the two there is a fixed and steady relation. An English gentleman, equally respectable for his rank and character, once observed to me, in the course of a private conversation, that, *whenever he looked at the wife of a bishop, he could not but smile*. Such is the feeling which, more or less, pervades every *Christian* heart. We know that Locke used formerly to call the bench of bishops the "*caput mortuum*" of the House of Lords. The primitive name exists, it is true; but then it is no more than a shadow of the former great, patriotic, and virtuous name which could shield a people's liberty, and make an impious tyrant tremble on his throne.

As to the mere parsons, it is scarcely worth while to notice them. The preacher of the faith is always respected, but the proclaimer of doubt is ever viewed in a ridiculous light. Wherever, therefore, doubt exists, its minister is ridiculed, and wherever he is so, skepticism will be found. Where, then, is faith? Peruse the debates on the Catholic Emancipation Bill,* (which was lost by a single vote,) and you will be surprised at the fallen favor and popularity of the Protestant *hierarchy* which appear in the discussion of so just, so righteous and holy a measure. One of the speakers even went so far as

---

* The day-star of religious freedom has at last emerged from the *reformation darkness* which had so long obscured it. A cruel and tyrannical government has been finally compelled to throw open the hall door of political equalization to the calumniated, enlightened, and patriotic Catholic. Protestant England never restored a portion of his natural and national right to the Catholic, whom she had so atrociously degraded and plundered, unless when really intimidated into the measure. The happy and glorious revolution of America, the unfortunate and disgraceful revolution of France, and, finally, the matchless, and mighty, and moral revolution lately effected in Ireland, by the illustrious O'Connell, the statesman, orator, patriot, and Catholic, were the mysterious means used by Providence to snap the tyrannical chains of heretical power, which for three centuries had paralyzed the energies of probably the bravest, most noble and generous nation in the world. The ferocious system of ungodly rule, from the days of the monster Henry VIII. to his present *worthy* successor on the throne of England, presents the philanthropist with an INQUISITION *indeed*, — an Inquisition for which the most fertile imagination cannot find a parallel in the great empire of fiction, and which, while it causes him to weep over the degradation of human nature, on the part of the oppressor, is calculated to wrest from him an unbounded admiration of the Catholic religion, that precious gift of God to man, for which so many millions had offered up their worldly goods, their brilliant prospects, their homes, and their lives, sooner than become renegades to the creed of their great ancestors, the apostles, and their Savior — God. — *Translator.*

to declare that *the house should not meddle wi[th] topics of that kind;* which, by the by, is somewh[at] strange, when an important question of religion [is] brought forward. In reality, he was right; for, fro[m] the moment that religion becomes a mere politic[al] engine, its ministers, *as such,* have nothing more [to] say. Such precisely is the case in England; *toler[a]tion,* upon which she has harped so long, *is not,* a[nd] *cannot be,* any other than a total indifference abo[ut] religion. The public prints and pamphlets of t[he] day noticed the death of some celebrated Englis[h] men, among whom was Charles Fox. He, in h[is] dying moments, put the following question to h[is] friends: "*What think ye of the soul? As for m[y] part,*" continued he, "*I believe it is immortal. [I] would believe so, even had Christianity never existe[d]; but to know what its condition will be after death f[ar] surpasses my comprehension.*" His great rival [in] fame soon followed him, and the details of his dea[th] also are before the public. A certain bishop, wh[o] had been his tutor, was known to pray at the bedsi[de] of the patient, who manifested no symptoms wha[t]ever of Christian edification or faith. I have parti[c]ularly noticed the dying scenes of these distinguishe[d] individuals, and I could never find a single positiv[e] act of faith, or truly Christian hope, connected wit[h] their awful *exit* from this stage of life.

We find in the letters of Madame Du Deffand [a] profession of the faith of her illustrious friend: "[I] believe," says he to this arrogant infidel, "*in a futu[re] life. God is so fond of dealing in the beautiful and the good, that we should confide in him for the remainder. We should not purposely offend him:* * *virtue must be pleasing to him, and we ought, therefore, to be virtuous, but our nature does not admit of perfection. God, therefore, does not require a perfection which is not natural. Such is my creed: it is very plain and exceedingly brief.* † *I have no fears, because He whom I serve is not a tyrant.*" ‡ Every sensible Englishman, of the Protestant faith, after a rigid self-examination, must acknowledge that his own creed is similar to that of the earl of Orford. §

Another proof of the indifference about religion in England is drawn from the apathy of the judiciary concerning crimes which are committed against the presumed faith of the land, yet which have occasionally seemed to open the eyes of the bench and awaken justice. Wollaston was formerly condemned to perpetual imprisonment for his *discourses on the Redeemer;* and we know that Eason was set

---

* The latent point of Jansenism, or Calvinistic malice, may be found in this expression; but provided a man does not act *precisely* with the view of offending the Deity, it may, so far, pass for a rational sentiment.

† This, however, is not the creed of the apostles, neither is it that of St. Athanasius, Nice, Constantinople, or Trent; it certainly is not the Confession of Augsburg, nor the faith of the Thirty-nine Articles, &c. &c.

‡ See Walpole's Letters to this lady.

§ Unless he secretly inclines to *another system;* and, in that case, it is an additional proof of my position.

in the pillory, about two years ago, for having attempted to upset the religion of the country.*

We should, however, be upon our guard: these men, and many more, whose fate I shall not pretend to decide, were, in every respect, what are commonly called profligate wretches, without fortune, principle, or protection.

It is possible that the constituted authorities may have felt a desire of making an experiment, as well as inflicting a merited punishment, upon such impious offenders; but, however unusual this may be, is it not obvious that the demoralizing *Bolingbroke*, lying *Hume*,† and infidel *Gibbon*, had acquired a

---

* See the *Morning Chronicle*, 5th June, 1812, Nos. 13, 441. It contains a letter, in which the writer, who blames the severity of the judges, and who signs himself *A true Christian*, proves, at least, that he is not *a true logician*, for he concludes with the following paradox: " *A religion can be destroyed*, but never supported, *by persecution ;* " as if it were possible to destroy a hostile system without supporting the religion which was opposed to it. It is just as if a man were to say that a certain medicine can remove a disease, but never preserve the health, or save the life, of the patient. It may be needless to remark that, in a late dictionary, the conduct of the judiciary, in defending the established religion of the state, is called *persecution.*

† Whilst on the subject of *Deism*, I shall take this opportunity of alluding to a circumstance in the death of the historian and philosopher, Mr. Hume, which has never yet been made properly clear. Hume is known to have professed and inculcated atheistical principles in several of his works, and has been represented by his biographers as an individual who, after having openly professed them through life, had the courage to maintain them to the end ; and, with the most *perfect composure* and tranquillity of mind, (equal to the boasted calmness of any Christian !) could take an affectionate leave of his friends, and drop into ETERNAL SLEEP!!! Such has been the extraordinary *miracle* operated by Mr. Hume in his last moments; and his deistical friends have been forward to represent it as a complete triumph over those taunts in which Christian orators are often disposed to indulge.

It should be observed that the preachers of the Christian religion

"damning fame," as well as the mammon of un-

have been uniformly in the habit of pointing to the death of infidels, and of contrasting their principles with their deportment in their last moments. They have appealed in particular to the death of Voltaire, who, notwithstanding the vigilance of persons about him, who were desirous of concealing what had passed, is known, by the evidence of his physician, to have exhibited on his death-bed the most shocking spectacle of raging despair that was ever witnessed. Hell itself, according to his account, could not present any thing more terrific. But Hume, the contemporary and rival of Voltaire, was to be an example of the contrary, and has been stated by philosophers to have died with the calmness and composure of a Christian saint! This, they say, *no one can contradict!* Such is their language. I have been too much accustomed to attend to the demands which our adversaries have never failed to make upon controvertists, of establishing *facts* by *proofs*, not to retaliate in this instance, and to require from these *deistical opponents* some *proofs*, before I admit the *fact* in question. There is a *sophism* in calling upon men to deny what has never been *proved*. *Denial*, as well as assertion, should be backed by *proof*. But, although it may be often difficult to *contradict* an assertion, silence is not to be construed into *admission*.

If, then, Mr. David Hume's death was tranquil and calm, as it has been described, where is the *evidence* — where are the *proofs?* As he quitted this life at Edinburgh, in the year 1776, if his death, as that of an undisguised atheist, was so *distinguished*, no doubt many of his friends were permitted to witness the miracle, and the *Christians*, above all, were led to the bedside of the dying atheist, to hear from his own lips some disquisition on the material elements of the human soul, when on the point of dissolving into chaos, as well as some moral reflections on the absolute extinction of vice and virtue in death, — all tending to confirm those *generous* and *noble* principles maintained by him through *public* life, and now sealed with his last breath. Surely, the public curiosity at Edinburgh, as well as through the world, was excited to know how Mr. Hume meant to die; and in all probability many requested to visit the expiring philosopher, that they might have the evidence of their own senses. Where, then, is their testimony collected? Where is the evidence of his servants, his household? Where are his *dying aphorisms*, minuted like those of Socrates of old? Where is his *written* testament, in his *own hand*, to be produced against the last confessions of so many Christian saints? I ask, where is the evidence — where are the proofs? There are none!!! What! are there none? And is the Christian expected to believe this *miracle* upon assertion?' There never was a question where *proofs* could have been more easily produced, if existing; there never was a question where they were more necessary; there never was a question more completely lost and *self-contradicted* with them. *We cannot deny it!!!* Now let us see what has been considered a *proof*, and what is the only evidence before the public. Nothing but a letter from Dr. Black to Dr. Adam Smith, introduced into the latter gen-

righteousness, by their blasphemous productions?

tleman's own account of Hume's last sickness, which was seemingly written with the special design of persuading the world that the philosopher had died with his atheistical principles unrecanted.

But Dr. Adam Smith must not think of imposing so easily on the sense of men. The last sentence of his letter, written three months after Hume's decease, sufficiently unveils his object in writing. "Upon the whole," he says, "I have always considered him, [Hume,] both in his lifetime and since his death, as approaching as nearly to the idea of a wise and virtuous man as perhaps the nature of human frailty will permit." What a blasphemous sentence for a Christian! Now, the fact is, that, notwithstanding Dr. Adam Smith lays considerable stress upon Hume's *cheerfulness* during his illness, telling the public that he amused himself in reading Lucian's "Dialogues of the Dead," and in joking about "Charon and his boat," (which, by the by, was not very philosophical at that time,) this epistolary biographer never saw Mr. Hume for better than a fortnight before he died. His last visit to him was on the 8th of August, 1776, when, going into the country, he left his patient at Edinburgh in the care of Dr. Black, who attended him till his death, which took place on the 25th of the same month. (*See Dr. Smith's published letter, usually printed at the head of Hume's History of England.*) Under these suspicious appearances have the circumstances of Hume's death continued nearly to this period, when Providence accidentally enabled me to throw in some new light upon the subject.

The late Governor Franklin, who died about two years ago at the advanced age of eighty, and who was son of the famous philosopher, Dr. Franklin, of America, had been the intimate friend of Hume, and was *present at his death.* This Governor Franklin, whose wife was a most pious Catholic, had in his family a young Catholic lady, a relation of Mrs. Franklin. This young lady, who died of a lingering decline a few months back, at about thirty years of age, was highly gifted with good sense and piety, and having addressed herself to me in quality of director, I became very intimately acquainted with her. I here suppress her name, because I have reason to believe it the wish of her friends that I should. Expressing her desire to me one day in conversation, that Governor Franklin might be brought to admit revealed religion before his death, she said she was the more astonished at his blindness, because he often spoke to her most feelingly of Hume's death, which had made a lasting impression upon his mind. Of course I requested her to repeat to me all she had heard from Governor Franklin on the subject, which she did without the smallest hesitation; and afterwards, at my desire, committed it to paper, and delivered it to me, declaring that it contained *the truth, and nothing but the truth.* I conversed with her on the subject, repeatedly, at different times, and I remarked that she never swerved in her statements. It was at length settled, with her full approbation, when she afterwards removed into the country, that I should attempt to obtain a confirmation of her account from Governor Franklin himself, by procuring an introduction to him. Yes, it

Has not *Hume** employed all the faculties of his perverted mind to upset every principle of truth, and the great, the only basis of morality?

---

was her opinion that I should not easily induce him to open himself to me. In the mean time, however, and on the very day that I addressed myself to a friend for this purpose, Governor Franklin was taken ill, and suddenly expired in his chair. To increase my disappointment in a matter so interesting to religion, the memorial of the young lady, his friend, was accidentally destroyed with other papers. No other resource therefore remained, but to apply to the same person for a *second* memorial, which she sent to me from the country, under her own hand, and dated January 18, 1814. To my questions, which may be gathered from her answers, she sent me the following statement, which she afterwards confirmed to me *orally* when under a decline: —

"I do not recollect the governor [Franklin] having ever mentioned the name of any person in particular, (present at the death of Hume.) He only said that the servants were in the room, and took particular care to deter any one from approaching the bed of death. He thought that this caution proceeded from their fears of having his wretched state of mind discovered. Probably the governor may have mentioned the same circumstances to some of his other friends which he did to me; but, if I recollect right, there was no one present when he spoke on the subject; and, in general, I should rather suppose he would avoid the subject, as striking to the very root of his own principles. For he assured me that nothing could give stronger evidence of the existence of a God, of the eternity of torments, of the worm of conscience, and of the blackest despair, than the very countenance of this unhappy man. It was curiosity, and a desire of seeing whether death, on the point of striking its blow, could shake those principles which he with so much care had for so long a time propagated and professed, that led the governor to him at that time; and it was their old intimacy and friendship which gained him admittance; for many were denied entrance into the house. He examined the state of his friend's *thoughts*, and found them in a truly lamentable situation. He endeavored to speak of God. Hume requested him to say no more; that he had grown old in, and so long propagated, his wretched principles, that it was now too late. The governor said something relative to his being a God of mercy, and ever ready to receive the returning criminal — but in vain; even the mention of *mercy* started the unhappy man, and made him appear to feel unutterable woe." — *Gandolphy's "Defence of the Ancient Faith,"* vol. iv. p. 446, 8vo. — *Translator.*

* In reference to lying Hume, I have derived the following anecdote from an aged, upright, and literary friend: —
Hume's father sent his *promising* son David to France, to complete his education. After a few years' residence in that delightful country, young Hume was so struck with the morality, intellect, and

Has he not — to use one of his many horrid and blasphemous remarks — publicly declared that *it is impossible for human reason to justify the character of God?** Has not Gibbon † asserted that, when J. J. Rousseau compared Socrates with Jesus Christ, (our divine and adorable Savior,) he *did not remark that the former had not suffered a word of impatience or despair to escape his lips?* Did not this diabolical expression, and many more of the

---

religion, of the people, that he became a Roman Catholic. This important conversion he communicated in one of his letters to his father, who immediately ordered him to return home. The father, on looking into the trunks of his son, found some Catholic prayer books in the portable library of the young convert, and indignantly exclaimed, "What! was it to become a Papist, or one of the pious Catholics, that I sent you to France? Is it thus you abused your time, wasted my money, and disappointed my expectations? I wanted to make a *gentleman*, a *statesman*, and *philosopher*, of you!" He then took the books and burned them in presence of the son, and in a few days sent him off to Switzerland, *to learn philosophy, and the elegant and useful qualifications of a gentleman of the world*, with a threat that, if he did not make a *good use* of his time, *he would be "cut off with a shilling."* David is placed in the hotbed of Calvinistic intolerance, his Christianity evaporates, and he now degenerates into a noxious weed in the garden of infidelity.

How many Catholics of this description could be here mentioned! How many are there, who, abusing the grace of God, and indifferent about the true Church, eventually become profligate and infamous, and, actuated by mean and mercenary motives, as well as instigated by distress, and the merited infamy into which they have fallen, ridicule and impiously rail at not only the Catholic clergy, but the Catholic Church, nay, the very adorable Head and Founder of the Church, Christ Jesus himself! Such wretches, like Voltaire of infamous memory, will, if they be not previously hurried off by suicide, as was *Rousseau*, call, in their death-bed moments, for a clergyman of the Catholic Church! But how many of them can now say that, unless they immediately repent and return to the Church of their pious and Catholic forefathers, they may not, like him, *call in vain*, and *die in despair*, in blasphemy of the Most High? — *Translator*.

* Essay on Liberty and Necessity. Beattie on Truth.

† See his History of the Decline and Fall of the Roman Empire, vol. xii. Paris, Maradan, 1794, chap. 47, pp. 9, 10.

kind which are to be found in his book, which is, in general, an anti-Christian system, bring him *more money* and *honor* (if the patronage and panegyric of an *unprincipled* and a *brutalized nobility*, and the *recommendation* of arrogant, superficial, and insipid philosophists, can be called *honor*) than he could have expected for any truly religious work, in which he might have eclipsed a Ditton, a Sherlock, or a Leland?

We should frankly confess that, when the tribunals of Britain, in their cowardly imbecility, or infidel apathy, do not arraign such outrageous and demoralizing offenders as a Bolingbroke, Hume, or Gibbon, before them, the laws are indeed strangely administered, especially when they afterwards fall with unsparing severity upon the heads of some poor and unpatronized wretches, who have not means enough to set them at defiance. In Gibbon's memoirs, we readily perceive the criminal and complimentary strain in which the *celebrated* Robertson indulges, when he writes to him concerning this selfsame work, which is so little thought of in this inconstant age — a book which, in reality, is a church history in disguise, and written not only by an arrogant infidel, but by a truly unprincipled and a very exceptionable individual.* Robertson appears

---

* Robertson wrote a letter to Gibbon, dated 12th May, 1781, in which he says, — "*I cannot conclude without telling you how much I approve of the reserve with which these new volumes have been written. I hope it will shelter you from the offensive and indecent criticism which the freedom of the former met with.*" Such an expression ought

in a still more criminal light, when he deals out his meed of praise to Voltaire, calling him, contrary to his conscience, both *wise* and *profound*; whereas there is no man, of sound reflection or extensive information, who does not know that Voltaire was a superficial smatterer, destitute of honesty, conscience, and shame.* This criminal eulogy has caused much and serious mischief to the world, by furnishing a seductive influence to the enemies of Christianity, who ever feel a silly as well as sinful vanity in lauding their ungodly champion, without ever giving themselves the trouble to inquire whether he spoke in earnest or in jest.

The truth is, that Robertson acted upon his *Scotch* proverb—"*Ca'e me, ca'e thee*"—when he thus made his servile court to Voltaire, with the expectation of being *puffed off* by him in turn. The more effectually to attain this object, he had recourse to a *celebrated* character, who was well qualified to act the part of a *go-between*.

This was the *pious* Du Deffand, who wrote to Voltaire in behalf of Robertson. "*He would wish,*" says this woman, "*to offer you the homage of his*

---

not to be expected from a divine, and a preacher of the Christian religion. *Priestley*, in his letter, 3d February, 1783, was not altogether so courteous.

"*I make no scruple,*" says he to Gibbon, "*in freely declaring it: your conduct is base and unbecoming. You insult the common sense of the Christian world. Defend, therefore, I say, not only your principles, but your honor. Can any thing be more dishonorable,*" &c. &c.

* Introduction to the History of Charles V. in 12mo. t. ii. sect. 3, note 44, p. 417.

works: I am commissioned to solicit your permission to that effect . . . . . His respect and veneration *for you are extreme."* *

What can we think of a member of the High Church of Scotland, of a doctor of divinity, and preacher of the Christian faith, who thus *respects* and *venerates* the most fiery, *notorious*, and profligate enemy of our heavenly religion?

Charity, it is true, and even politeness, are perfectly independent of the symbols of faith, and we should, notwithstanding, most strictly observe them; but then *there is a line marked out by conscience.* Bergier would assuredly have rendered to all the miscreants whom he had refuted in the course of his long and precious life all the service, at a suitable time, which lay in his power; and it is very remarkable that the most insulting attacks which had been made upon him never drew a single sarcasm from him; yet he was very far from speaking of Freret and Voltaire in terms of *respect* and *veneration.* Such a compliment, however, should have disgraced a High Church clergyman. Robertson could carelessly flatter and fawn upon Gibbon and Voltaire; for the *state* Christianity which he preached was, in his opinion, only an improved and edifying mythology, which he could twist and fashion as he thought best adapted to his purpose. His last work *reveals the grand secret;* and, notwith-

---

* See her letters to Voltaire, in 8vo. vol. iv. 20th Dec. 1760, p. 320.

standing all the precaution he had taken to the contrary, there is no intelligent reader who will not come to the conclusion that Robertson was a consummate infidel.*

Perhaps you may be curious enough to know the sentiments of another English doctor on the nature of original sin, and man's degradation, which must be considered as the basis of Christianity: —"*Father Malebranche,*" observes Dr. Beattie, "*informs us that the senses were originally very honest faculties, and such as might be desired, until they were debauched by original sin—a circumstance which gave them an invincible disposition to deceive us, so that they are at the present day ever on their sharps to play off their tricks upon us.*"

I have hitherto confined myself to England, because she is the very head and front, and as some have stupidly called her, the bulwark, of Protestantism.† Were I to direct my observations to another

---

* Robertson's Historical Account, &c. Basle, 1792, in 8vo. appendix.

† What the pious Bishop Challoner said in his *caveat* against *Methodists*, is strictly applicable to the root, trunk, and branches, of the system commonly called the *reformation*.

The *reformation* sects are not the people of God; they are not true gospel Christians; nor is their newly-raised society the true Church of Christ, or any part of it.

All this is clearly demonstrated by undeniable evidence of the word of God, from innumerable texts, both of the Old and New Testament, marking out to us the people of God, in the society of the true Church of Christ, by such characters as can by no means agree with the *reformation* sects, or any other newly-raised sect or communion.

The Old Testament is full of illustrious prophecies, relating to the Church of Christ; that is to say, to the people of God, under the law of Christ. The New Testament is no less explicit, in the glorious

quarter, I may be supposed to transcend the limits which I originally proposed to myself; I cannot,

---

promises it makes, and the glorious character it gives to this same Church or society of Christ.

The prophecies of the Old Testament concerning the Church of Christ may be seen, Isaiah, c. ii. v. 2, And in the last days the mountain of the house of the Lord shall be prepared on the top of mountains, and it shall be exalted above the hills; and all nations shall flow unto it. — c. ix. v. 6, For a child is born to us; and a son is given to us; and the government is upon his shoulders; and his name shall be called Wonderful, Counsellor, God the Mighty, the Father of the world to come, the Prince of peace. His empire shall be multiplied; and there shall be no end of peace : He shall sit upon the throne of David, and upon his kingdom; to establish it, and strengthen it with judgment and with justice, from henceforth and forever: the zeal of the Lord of hosts will perform this. — c. xxxv. v. 4, Say to the faint hearted, Take courage, and fear not: behold, your God will bring the revenge of recompense: God himself will come, and will save you. — v. 5, Then shall the eyes of the blind be opened; and the ears of the deaf shall be unstopped. — v. 8, And a path and a way shall be there; and it shall be called the holy way; the unclean shall not pass over it; and this shall be unto you a straight way, so that fools shall not err therein. — c. liv. v. 1, Give praise, O thou barren, that bearest not; sing forth praise, and make a joyful noise, thou that didst not travail with child; for many are the children of the desolate, more than of her that hath a husband, saith the Lord. — v. 2, Enlarge the place of thy tent, and stretch out the skins of thy tabernacles: spare not, lengthen thy cords, and strengthen thy stakes. — v. 9, This thing is to me as in the days of Noe, to whom I swore that I would no more bring in the waters of Noe upon the earth: so have I sworn not to be angry with thee, and not to rebuke thee. — v. 10, For the mountains shall be moved, and the hills shall tremble; but my mercy shall not depart from thee, and the covenant of my peace shall not be moved, said the Lord, that hath mercy on thee. — v. 13, All thy children shall be taught of the Lord; and great shall be the peace of thy children. — v. 17, No weapon that is formed against thee shall prosper; and every tongue that resisteth thee in judgment thou shalt condemn. This is the inheritance of the servants of the Lord, and their justice with me, saith the Lord. — c. lix. v. 19, And they from the west shall fear the name of the Lord, and they from the rising of the sun his glory; when he shall come as a violent stream, which the Spirit of the Lord driveth on. — v. 20, And there shall come a Redeemer to Sion, and to them that return from iniquity in Jacob, saith the Lord. — v. 21, This is my covenant with them, saith the Lord: my Spirit that is in thee, and my words that I have put in thy mouth, shall not depart out of thy mouth, nor out of the mouth of thy seed, nor out of the mouth of thy seed's seed, saith the Lord, from henceforth and forever. — c. li. v. 2, To proclaim the accept-

however, resist the temptation which I feel to devi-

able year of the Lord, and the day of vengeance of our God; to comfort all that mourn. — v. 3, To appoint to the mourners of Sion, and to give them a crown for ashes, the oil of joy for mourning, a garment of praise for the spirit of grief: and they shall be called in it The mighty ones of justice, the planting of the Lord, to glorify *him*. — v. 11, For as the earth bringing forth her bud, and as the garden causeth her seed to shoot forth, so shall the Lord God make justice to spring forth, and praise before all the nations. — c. lxii. v. 1, For Sion's sake I will not hold my peace, and for the sake of Jerusalem I will not rest, till her just One come forth as brightness, and her Savior be lighted as a lamp. — v. 2, And the Gentiles shall see thy just One, and all kings thy glorious One; and thou shalt be called by a new name, which the mouth of the Lord shall name. — v. 4, Thou shalt no more be called Forsaken; and thy land shall no more be called Desolate; but thou shalt be called My pleasure in her, and thy land inhabited: because the Lord hath been well pleased with thee; and thy land shall be inhabited. — v. 6, Upon thy walls, O Jerusalem, I have appointed watchmen all the day, and all the night they shall never hold their peace. You that are mindful of the Lord, hold not your peace, &c.

Jeremiah, c. xxxi. v. 31, Behold, the days shall come, saith the Lord, and I will make a new covenant with the house of Israel, and with the house of Juda. — v. 35, Thus saith the Lord, who giveth the sun for the light of the day, the order of the moon and of the stars for the light of the night; who stirreth up the sea, and the waves thereof roar: the Lord of hosts is his name. — v. 36, If these ordinances shall fail before me, saith the Lord, then also the seed of Israel shall fail, so as not to be a nation before me forever. — v. 37, Thus saith the Lord: If the heavens above can be measured, and the foundations of the earth searched out beneath, I also will cast away all the seed of Israel, for all that they have done, saith the Lord. — c. xxxiii. v. 14, Behold, the days come, saith the Lord, that I will perform the good word that I have spoken to the house of Israel, and to the house of Juda. — v. 17, For thus saith the Lord: There shall not be cut off from David a man to sit upon the throne of the house of Israel. — v. 20, Thus saith the Lord: If my covenant with the day can be made void, and my covenant with the night, that there should not be day and night in their season. — v. 21, Also my covenant with David my servant may be made void, that he should not have a son to reign upon his throne, and with the Levites and priests, my ministers.

Ezechiel, c. xxxvii. v. 24, And my servant David shall be king over them; and they shall have one shepherd: they shall walk in my judgments, and shall keep my commandments, and shall do them.

Daniel, c. ii. v. 34, Thus thou sawest, till a stone was cut out of a mountain without hands; and it struck the statue upon the feet thereof, that were of iron and of clay, and broke them in pieces. — v. 35, Then was the iron, the clay, the brass, the silver, and the gold, broken to pieces together, and became like the chaff of a summer's

ate a little, in order to lay before you a profession of

threshing-floor; and they were carried away by the wind; and there was no place found for them: but the stone that struck the statue became a great mountain, and filled the whole earth. — v. 44, But in the days of those kingdoms the God of heaven will set up a kingdom that shall never be destroyed: and his kingdom shall not be delivered up to another people: and it shall consume all these kingdoms; and itself shall stand forever.

The promises made to the Church of Christ, and the glorious characters given to it in the New Testament, are found St. Matthew, c. xvi. v. 18, And I say to thee, That thou art Peter, and upon this rock I will build my church; and the gates of hell shall not prevail against it. — c. xviii. v. 17, And if he will not hear them, tell the church. And if he will not hear the church, let him be to thee as the heathen and the publican. — v. 18, Amen, I say unto you, Whatsoever you shall bind upon earth shall be bound also in heaven, and whatsoever you shall loose upon earth shall be loosed also in heaven. — c. xxviii. v. 18, And Jesus, coming, spoke to them, saying, All power is given to me, in heaven and in earth. — v. 19, Go ye, therefore, and teach all nations; baptizing them in the name of the Father, and of the Son, and of the Holy Ghost. — v. 20, Teaching them to observe all things whatsoever I have commanded you; and, behold, I am with you all days, even to the consummation of the world.

St. Luke, c. i. v. 33, And of his kingdom there shall be no end. — c. x. v. 16, He that heareth you, heareth me; and he that despiseth you, despiseth me. And he that despiseth me, despiseth him that sent me.

St. John, c. x. v. 16, And other sheep I have, that are not of this fold: them also I must bring; and they shall hear my voice: and there shall be made one fold and one Shepherd. — c. xiv. v. 16, And I will ask the Father, and he shall give you another Paraclete, that he may abide with you forever. — v. 17, The Spirit of truth, whom the world cannot receive; because it seeth him not, nor knoweth him: but you shall know him; because he shall abide with you, and shall be in you. — v. 26, But the Paraclete, the Holy Ghost, whom the Father will send in my name, he will teach you all things, and bring all things to your mind, whatsoever I shall have said to you. — c. xvi. v. 13, But when he, the Spirit of truth, shall come, he will teach you all truth; for he shall not speak of himself; but what things soever he shall hear, he shall speak; and the things that are to come he will show you.

Ephes. c. v. v. 11, And some, indeed, he gave to be apostles, and some prophets, and others evangelists, and others pastors and teachers. — v. 23, For the husband is the head of the wife, as Christ is the head of the church. He is the Savior of his body. — v. 24, Therefore, as the church is subject to Christ, so also let the wives be to their husbands, in all things.

1 Timothy, c. iii. v. 14, These things I write to thee, hoping that I shall come to thee shortly. — v. 15, But if I tarry long, that thou mayest know how thou oughtest to behave thyself in the house of

faith of the *famous* Herder, an *evangelical bishop*.

God, which is the church of the living God, the pillar and ground of the truth.

Now all these prophecies, all these promises, all these glorious characters, set down in the Scriptures, relating to the Church of Christ, or the people of God of the New Testament, evidently point out to us a *society* founded by Christ himself, with all power and authority from him, and by his commission propagated far and near throughout the world — a *society* which, from this beginning, should ever flourish, till time itself should end ; ever *one*, ever *holy*, ever *orthodox ; founded upon a rock ; proof against all the powers of hell ;* secured against error by the *perpetual presence* and assistance of *Christ*, her *King*, her *Shepherd*, and her *Spouse ;* who is the *way, the truth,* and the *life ;* ever taught and directed by his Spirit, the *Holy Ghost, the Spirit of truth :* furnished by him with a perpetual succession of church guides, pastors, and teachers, divinely appointed and divinely assisted ; favored by a solemn oath of God himself, promising his *peace and loving-kindness forever*, and assured by him that his *Spirit*, the pure profession of his *words*, his *light*, and his *sanctuary*, should be with her. forevermore. Such is evidently the Scripture character of Christ's Church, and of the true society of gospel Christians, or the people of God of the New Testament. As, then, it is visible that no part of this character is applicable to the *reformation* sects, who have no succession from, nor communion with, that original, never-failing, *one, holy, catholic*, and *apostolical* society, founded by Christ, and descending from him, it must be evident that they cannot possibly be any part of the people of God, or true gospel Christians.

In a word, the society of the true people of God, under the gospel dispensation, is, according to the Scriptures, a society founded by Christ *upon a rock*, ever subsisting and victorious over death and hell, ever *one, holy,* and *apostolical ;* but the *reformation* sects, who were never heard of for fifteen hundred years after Christ, are no such society, nor have any communion with any such society : therefore the *reformation* sects are no part of the people of God ; they are no gospel Christians.

Hence it follows that they have no share in the Scriptures, nor any right to apply to themselves any of those Scripture texts which were addressed to the people of God, or to the true children of the Church of Christ ; for they were not designed for them, nor written to them. *We know*, says the apostle, Rom. iii. 19, *that what things soever the law saith, it saith to them that are under the law.* So, in like manner, what things are spoken in the *New Testament*, are spoken to the children of the *New Testament*, the one, Holy, Catholic, and Apostolical Church of Christ : the *reformation* sects have no share in them ; they are quite out of the question.

The reformation teachers are not the true ministers of Christ ; nor are they called or sent by him.

This follows from what has been already demonstrated ; for, if the *reformation* sects, as we have seen above, are not the true people of Christ, their ministers, of course, cannot be the true ministers of Christ.

The same is further proved, because the true ministers of Christ can be no others than such as come down by succession from the apostles of Christ. But the *reformation* teachers do not come down from the apostles of Christ. Therefore they are not the true ministers of Christ; and, consequently, they have no manner of power or commission from him, to bless in his name, or to preach his word, or to administer his sacraments.

All spiritual power, jurisdiction, and authority, in the Church of Christ, must come from him, and cannot be executed without a criminal presumption and usurpation, any otherwise than by *commission* from him; so that whosoever intrudes himself, *of his own head*, into the pastoral office, or any of the spiritual functions of the Church, in the language of the Scripture, is a *thief* and a *robber*, St. John x. 1. Now, there are but two ways that this divine *commission* (without which it would be high treason against God to usurp the office or functions of his delegates and ministers) can be imparted to any person, viz., either immediately, by God himself, as he sent Moses and the prophets in the Old Testament, and Christ and his apostles in the New; or else by being licensed and empowered by men who have that authority handed down to them from those who were originally *commissioned* by God; of which kind are the mission and calling of the ordinary pastors of the Church of Christ, deriving their spiritual power, jurisdiction, and authority, from the apostles, who were commissioned by Christ himself: *as my Father sent me, I send you*, St. John xx., with a promise of his abiding with them and with their successors forever. *Lo, I am with you always, even to the end of the world*, Matt. xviii. 20.

Now, the *reformation* teachers have no share at all in this divine *commission*: it has not been imparted to them in either of these ways. They have not that *extraordinary mission* immediately from God himself, as *Moses* and the prophets, *Christ* and the apostles, had; because they cannot (as *they* did) produce their *patents*, stamped with the broad seal of heaven. They could never yet work any one evident miracle in proof of their being the extraordinary delegates of God; for God would not have us to receive any, as immediately sent from him, without their producing their proper credentials, signed and sealed by him: otherwise, we might be daily exposed to the danger of *false prophets*, and *wolves in sheep's clothing*, who never fail to boast of the *Spirit*, and to cry out, "*The Lord, the Lord*," though *the Lord* never sent them. So that we have a right to conclude that such as cannot produce extraordinary proofs of their being sent, in an extraordinary manner, immediately from God himself, were, indeed, never sent in this manner by him; since God's sending his delegates to men necessarily implies an obligation in men to receive those whom he sends; which obligation could by no means take place where these pretended delegates could

some German book, the *Bossuet of Germany!*

not produce their credentials. Therefore the *reformation* teachers, who can produce no such proof of their immediate mission from God himself, have, in effect, received no such extraordinary commission from him.

Neither have these new teachers any share in the *ordinary mission*, or *vocation*, of God's ministers, derived by succession from *Christ's* first commissioners, the apostles, through the channel of the Church; for none of the undoubted successors of the apostles in *Christ's* Church ever imparted this commission to the *reformation* sects; none of them ever sent, or authorized them to preach; they stand divided in communion from all churches that have any pretension to antiquity; their doctrine of justification by faith alone, in the manner they maintain it, was anathematized, at its first appearance, by the undoubted heirs of the apostles, the pastors of the apostolic Church: therefore they could have no commission from them, or through them, to preach, or teach, or execute any of the pastoral functions; and, consequently, they preach without being sent at all from God, either in the ordinary or extraordinary way: they have intruded themselves into the ministry, *of their own* head; and are sent by no other than by him who sent all the false prophets from the beginning.

The reformation teachers have not the marks by which the Scripture would have us to know the true ministers of Christ; nor do their fruits, in any respect, resemble those of the first teachers of Christianity.

First, Because, as we have seen in our preceding numbers, they preach without *being sent*, contrary to the apostle, Rom. x. 15. They have *taken the honor* of the pastoral ministry *to themselves, without being called of God, as was Aaron*, Heb. v. 4. They *enter not into the sheepfold by the door, but climb up another way;* which is the mark given by our Lord of *thieves* and *robbers*, St. John x. 1.

Secondly, Because they refuse to submit their preaching to the trial of the ordinary pastors, succeeding the apostles in the government of Christ's Church; which is an evident mark that *they are not of God:* according to the beloved disciple, 1 John iv. 6, *He that knoweth God, heareth us,* [the apostles and their successors;] *he that is not of God, heareth not us: by this we know the spirit of truth, and the spirit of error.*

Thirdly, Because, under the *sheep's clothing*, which they put on, they bring not forth *the fruits* by which our Lord would have us know and discern his true ministers, from the *false prophets*, of whom he admonishes us to beware, St. Matt. vii. 15. By the *sheep's clothing* is meant an outward show of religion, a fair outside, a formal cant, interlarded with scraps of Scripture, wrested to serve a wicked purpose; much boasting of the *Spirit*, and of the *truth*, and crying out, " *The Lord, the Lord;* " whilst both the *Lord* and his *Spirit* are far from their hearts, and his *truth* is not amongst them. This

Hear, then, sir, what this *father of a Protestant*

has been more or less the character of all *false prophets*, from the beginning; they have generally put on the *sheep's clothing*; they have all pretended to godliness; they have all quoted the Scriptures, and *boasted of the Spirit*, and, being, indeed, no better than *ministers of Satan*, have endeavored to make themselves appear as the *ministers of righteousness*, 1 Cor. xi. 15. But their fruits have always betrayed them; such as those the apostle describes, (1 Tim. iv. 2; 2 Tim. iii. 2, 5, 16,) viz., that *they speak lies in hypocrisy; that they are lovers of themselves, covetous*, (that is, *lovers of money,) boasters, proud,* (preaching up themselves,) *having a form of godliness, but denying the power thereof; that they creep into houses, and take captive silly women laden with sins; ever learning, and never able to come to the knowledge of the truth;* and who, by a just judgment of God, are given up to a *strong delusion, that they should believe a lie;* because they *would not receive the love of the truth, that they might be saved*, 2 Thes. ii. 10.

But how different were the *fruits* by which the apostles, and the other first preachers of Christianity, showed themselves to be the true ministers of Christ! Like their great Master, they were *meek and humble of heart; they preached not themselves,* but *Christ crucified;* they made no boast of themselves, nor began with publishing the *pretended dealings of God with them*, or the journals of their own travels and labors; for they *sought not their own glory*, but purely the glory of their Master. They were *poor in spirit*, and poor in effects, too; for *silver and gold they had none*, Acts iii. 6. They were no lovers of *this mammon of unrighteousness;* they *laid up no treasures upon earth;* they married no rich fortunes; they had no bankers, or cashkeepers; they built no stately palaces, to hold forth in; they kept no coaches, nor horses; they were perfectly disinterested, with regard to filthy lucre; they *devoured not the houses of widows, under pretext of long prayer*, Matt. xxiii. 14; they neither exacted nor received from the faithful what they could not give without detriment to their families; much less did they suffer wives to give to them the substance of their husbands, &c. But *giving no offence in any thing, that their ministry might not be blamed, they approved themselves in all things, as the ministers of God, in much patience, in afflictions, in necessities, in distresses, in stripes, in imprisonments, in tumults, in labors, in watchings, in fastings, by pureness (and chastity,) by knowledge, by long-suffering, by kindness, by the Holy Ghost, by love unfeigned, by the word of truth, by the armor of justice, on the right hand and on the left*, &c., 2 Cor. vi. Such were the fruits they showed forth in themselves.

As to the fruits which, by their preaching, they produced in others, they were manifest to the whole world, in the saintly lives of their converts, the primitive Christians. Their doctrine perpetually inculcated the necessity of penance, as well as of faith; of a thorough conversion of sinners from their evil ways; of a change of heart, and of a change of life; of *keeping all the commandments*, in *order to obtain life everlasting;* of not trusting to faith alone; but joining

church asserts.* "Every thing on our globe is given to rotation and change. Where is the man, who, if he duly consider the circular figure of the earth, can be led away by the idea of converting the whole world to the same verbal creed, † in philosophy or

---

with their faith *good works,* and *continuing in goodness to the end.* They drove none into despair by their preaching; *the bruised reed they did not break;* and *the smoking flax they did not extinguish;* neither did they preach up to any persons, under the name of *faith,* a *presumptuous assurance* of their own justification and eternal salvation by faith alone; but, rather, they exhorted all men to *work out their salvation with fear and trembling,* Phil. ii. 12. To labor, by *good works, to make their election sure,* 2 Pet i. 13. Telling them that *he who thinketh himself to stand, must take heed lest he fall,* 1 Cor. x. 12. That such as are *ingrafted* in the stock, and now *stand by faith,* must *not be highminded, but fear,* lest otherwise they be *cut off,* and perish everlastingly, Rom. xi. 20, 21, 22. That such as are now in grace must take care *to hold fast that which they have,* lest another *take their crown,* Rev. iii. 11. That they that run in the Christian race, or that strive for the mastery, must so run, and so fight, as to obtain the prize; but never to think themselves secure till the race is over, and the fight is at an end, after the example of the great apostle himself, who in this warfare thought it necessary *to chastise his body, and bring it into subjection; lest by any means, after having preached to others, he himself should be a castaway,* 1 Cor. ix. 26, 27. Can any one be so presumptuous as to think himself more secure than the apostle? Surely, such as disdain this humble fear must have been given up, in punishment of the pride of their hearts, to an incurable blindness, by Him who ever *resists the proud, and to the humble gives his grace,* 1 Pet. v. 5.

By this contrast between the true ministers sent by Christ, to preach his gospel, and the false prophets, who seek to impose upon us, by the *sheep's clothing,* and so beguile us of our faith; and between the different fruits which each sect produces, the one very good, and the other very evil; it will be easy for any sincere Christian, who loves the truth, and desires not to be deceived, to pronounce judgment in the present case, whether these new teachers are to be received, as bearing the marks, and producing the fruits, of the primitive and apostolic preachers, or to be rejected, as resembling much more the *false prophets,* and bringing forth fruits which can never come from a good tree, even the very worst of fruits, such as an incurable pride, self-conceit, presumption, contempt of all others, and slander of Catholicity and its ministers — evils most hateful to God, and most pernicious to the souls of men. — *Translator.*

* Herder's *Ideen* zur Philosophie der Geschichte der Menschheit, t. i. chap. iv. p. 23.

† *Wortglauben.* — If this difference consisted merely in *words,* it

religion, or of *cutting its throat* through stupid, yet holy, zeal? The rapid revolutions of a ball are a strong resemblance of every thing that passes on our planet."

Such an argument against the unity and universality of our religion, and the productive labors of Catholic missioners, is novel indeed, and worthy of the Bossuet * of *Germany!* An English critic hereupon started an inquiry, whether it would be equally absurd to cut one's throat, in support of philosophical or religious opinions, on a conical or cylindrical planet.

It is hard to say. Now, sir, allow me to ask you, when a *preacher* of this kind ascends his pulpit, is it not natural to suppose that every member of the audience will say to himself, "Who knows whether this *fellow* himself believes in what he is going to preach to me?" What confidence can such *teachers*

---

may not be considered a rash or Quixotic measure to attempt to reclaim mankind, neither would there arise any serious calamity to society, if the measure did not succeed. Herder was determined to be impious, even at the expense of accuracy.

* What consolation must it not be to each spiritual successor of St. Peter, nay, to the whole hierarchy and laity of the Catholic world, to reflect that, from the anti-social and *dark age* of the pseudo-reformation to the present day, a single village or hamlet has not been converted to the religion of the cross in any part of the universe by any of the anti-Catholic sects, notwithstanding the mercenary scribbling, *concerted* "*revivals*," Protean plots, conspiracies, and *societies*, which "the children of this world," in all their wisdom and cunning, have formed and matured against the Apostolic Church of the Divine Jesus! Is not such a phenomenon calculated to furnish an inexhaustible theme of inquiry to the true philanthropist, philosopher, politician, and patriot? How many millions of lives and of pounds sterling, what splendid proofs of genius and industry, have not disappeared under the destructive wheels of the gigantic Juggernaut of the *reformation!* — *Translator.*

inspire? Must not the audience, on the contrary, feel a sovereign contempt for them, and even extend it to the doctrine of all such spiritual quacks? Undoubtedly. The consistent and sensible, after having read the flimsy and incoherent productions of such mountebanks, whose primary maxim is a contempt for all authority, must be even shocked at the reiteration of their heretical jargon, and, by not only disbelieving it, but also frowning upon the *lawfulness* of their mission, cannot conceive how any man can question so inseparable a connection.

Theory and experience satisfactorily prove that *there is not*, that *there cannot be, a steady faith, or positive religion*, properly so called, in a nation whose envoys take so much pains to abolish what they and others, through malice, call the *detestable Inquisition*.

Christianity is so far effaced in England, that, some short time ago, certain individuals, when a cobweb thread *secured* them to the ancient faith, had reason to fear that Indifference, under the deceptive mask of toleration, would eventually give rise, in Britain, to legislators who might be totally estranged from Christianity. When they saw the Christian tenets rapidly disappearing, they wished at least to make sure of the capital dogma of the Trinity, without which Christianity does not, cannot, exist; and they accordingly brought forward the *Trinity-Doctrine Bill*, by virtue whereof every English subject, who would refuse to swear to this fundamental article of the Christian faith, should be disqualified as a member of parliament. The framers and movers of the bill had evidently shown their prudence, and still nothing less could be expected from persons who manifested any, even the slightest, attachment to a Christian character. Parliament, nevertheless, found that such a requisite would not do; and the members of the House at that time felt, in their conscience, that they had not a right to restrict the conscientious impressions of candidates, however infidel and destructive the tendency of such impressions may be. They, therefore, very cautiously and consistently avoided taxing any future candidate with an oath which they themselves would not take, and they accordingly threw out the bill. Thus an Englishman, were he of the Arian heresy, or Mahometan- school, becomes (*cæteris paribus*) eligible to a seat in parliament, since there is no intelligent Turk who would refuse to acknowledge Christ as a very honest man, nay, even as a great prophet.

On this occasion, a witty writer in the MORNING CHRONICLE of Nov. 11, 1814, could not resist the temptation of composing the following epigram upon the imperial parliament:—

> Kings, lords, and commons, do decree
> That, henceforth, every man is free
> To think, or say, as it may be,
> That one is one, and three are three.

Please to remember, sir, that the absurd toleration of England extends only to sectarianism, and by no means to the Holy Catholic Church ! ! In relation to her, the English laws are of the most grinding, oppressive character, and in every respect, from their iniquitous effects, calculated to endanger the government. A Protestant Englishman will not have a system which requires an increase of faith; but let any mountebank devise a would-be religious scheme of belief, and confine it to a few articles, and the poor Englishman will eagerly receive it !

The act of parliament church of Britain swarms with non-conforming sects, that prey and fatten on it. They leave it only an external form, which the Episcopalians, through indifference, interest, or ignorance, seem to take, or, in truth, do take, for something real.

METHODISM, or the sect best known in genteel society in Great Britain and Ireland by the name of SWADDLING, invades every state and condition, and now openly menaces to deluge the national religion of England. An English writer proposes a singular plan to oppose the torrent of this heretical innovation. "If evil," says he, "makes additional progress, the English Church may find it necessary to use some degree of indulgence in relation to her articles of faith, and receive within her pale a larger number of Christians!" Such an expedient is laughable in the extreme. It is just as if this *sapient* writer, in order to exterminate *Swaddling*, or *Methodism*, would have the Church of England, *which is founded upon acts of parliament*, to remit the merit of *good works* to the *Puritan* offspring of Calvin, the sacraments to the Quakers, the Trinity to the Arians, &c. &c. !!

Then, forsooth, the Protestant church of the "thorough-godly reformation" will raise an invincible phalanx of *biblical* soldiers for the extermination of Methodism! Such a *pious*, vast, and *noble* design, is worthy of the philosophy and Christianity of a refined *reformation!*

The projector of this admirable plan for the reënforcement of the English Church *militant* is, no doubt, "both loyal and true:" he reasons according to the principles of conscience and the general impression of his *pious* neighbors. Of what use are religious tenets to such persons? The Apostles' Creed becomes nugatory; it is swallowed up in the impetuous and confluent tides of prejudice and passion. The Church of England no longer exists as a religious establishment, or spiritual power. The weight of two centuries has already crushed into dust and ashes the trunk of that withered tree: the external bark alone can be traced, because the state authority, by means of British bayonets, conceives it political to secure and guard the ground on which it fell.

You must, sir, have been really astonished that a once great and Christian nation should object to the necessary qualifications of a Christian in a legislative member! But how great will be your surprise when I lay before you "a something more *exquisite still*"? Were I to tell you that England had *solemnly*, I had almost said *officially*, renounced Christianity, you would immediately exclaim, that my assertion was paradoxical; I can assure you, sir, that I do present you with a paradox; but is that a reason why I should not give it publicity?

Cicero himself has recorded *six* strange things in his day; and why will you not allow me the privilege of mentioning *one*?

I therefore request that you will attentively peruse it. You will find it in my next letter, and we shall then — as *you know* that I am not made up of the *sternest stuff* — endeavor to adjust all differences, and regulate matters in such a way as will eventually bear out the truth of my position.

Meantime, sir, believe me to be,

Yours, &c. &c.

Moscow, Aug. 19, 1815.

LETTER VI.

Sir,

Who has not heard of David Hume? *Cui non notus Hylas?* Taking every thing into consideration, I do believe that the eighteenth century, so remarkably productive of infidelity, never gave birth to so heartless and inveterate an enemy to the Church of Christ.

The cold but corrosive poison of that atheist was much more dangerous than the effervescing venom of Voltaire, who was occasionally known to express some sort of respect for fundamental truths, and to allow that

> *Si Dieu n'existait pas, il faudrait l'inventer;*
> A God we should invent, if one did not exist.

Even the wretched Voltaire was less criminal than the wicked Hume. The present occasion, however, will not permit me to assign my reasons; but the palpable contradictions which strike the conscience of the reader render Voltaire much less dangerous than the Scotch infidel, who endeavored to sap the foundation of truth with all the cold-blooded wickedness of a Calvin, and the imperturbable composure of a logician. He declared, as we have already remarked, that "it is impossible to justify the character of God;" and, moreover, asserts, that to "free the Deity from being the author of sin, has been found hitherto to exceed all the powers of philosophy." To what iniquitous sophistry has he not had recourse in order to upset every idea of liberty, to annihilate the very basis of morality? The human mind, however well trained, and guarded against such insidious considerations, is very apt to yield under the accumulated sophistry of this seductive writer. The intelligent reader feels that Hume is wrong, even before he can assign his reasons for so thinking. If among the sons of men, who have ever heard the divine gospel explained, there was an unmixed atheist, — which I take not upon myself to decide, — Hume was that man. I never perused his anti-religious works without shuddering, and asking myself, "How is it possible that a man, so amply possessed of the means of acquiring the truth, could so far insult the dignity of nature, and degrade the noble powers of the human understanding?" I have ever been of opinion that the moral obduracy of Hume, and his insolent serenity, were the certain punishment of a rebel against the light of mind — a crime against which mercy bars the gates of heaven, and for which Deity thus punishes the sinner, by totally withdrawing his sacred influence from him.

When Hume speaks of primary truths, as we have just seen, it is evident that he gives himself very little trouble about the practical duties of Christianity, and no one will therefore be surprised at his keen and characteristic irony in the following passage: "So that, upon the whole, we may conclude that the *Christian religion* not only was at first attended with miracles, but even at this day cannot be believed by any reasonable person without one. Mere reason is insufficient to convince us of its veracity; and whoever is moved by *faith* to assent to it, is conscious of a continued miracle in his own person, which subverts all the principles of his understanding, and gives him a determination to believe what is most contrary to custom and experience!"

This man, notwithstanding, led a tranquil life in the midst of ease, and of every distinction which genius commands! This, in itself, and as we have noticed in a preceding letter, evidently shows that in England, as elsewhere, *cobwebs are made for flies*. What is still more curious, the honors which were conferred upon his memory have far surpassed the consideration and respect which he had enjoyed during his iniquitous career; for the king and both houses of parliament have solemnly accepted the dedication of the splendid edition of his History of England, which has not long since been ushered into the literary market. Had the legislature refused such a tribute from no other motive (if I be allowed the expression) than that of chastising the memory of a mortal enemy to their national religion, they would have acted in character. The English *hierarchy* have been more than once censured for having hurled their anathemas against this author; but, sir, on a careful examination, I am sure you will not condemn them for it.

There is no law whose perfect equity is so unexceptionably admitted as that which punishes the culprit *for his crime*. Morality and justice equally concur in the belief *that he who abuses the gifts of genius should be deprived of its recompense*. Had this been immovably established and rigidly enforced, as a law of the land, it would have prevented many a revolting abuse. It is a crying shame for the French nation, and the century in which it occurred, that the infamous author of *Joan of Arc* had not locked the gates of the French Academy against the author of *Zaire*, or had not forever expelled him from that literary society.

Let us suppose that Hume had been condemned to death, or even arraigned at the bar of his country, for one of those crimes which, according to the *black statute* book, are punishable with death; would not many of those offences which that code deems capital, (for instance, the stealing of a sheep, or any article of the value of a *shilling*,) be less criminal, in the eyes of eternal Justice, than his demoralizing works, wherein he so obstinately and impiously attacks the most sacred dogmas of natural and revealed religion, and whereby he endeavors to convulse and confound the Christian universe? Even with such an impression on their minds, I am satisfied that the Protestant and truly fallible head of the English Church, and his *ministerial* parliament, would not refuse the dedicatory homage of this infidel's history.

If, then, they accepted it, (and who doubts it?) must it not have been owing to the *friendly* view which they had taken of his *anti-religious* writings; and that they still consider the Protestant religion as a mere speculative opinion, upon which they pronounced their *yeas*, or *nays*, with the same indifference that they would upon any question of natural philosophy or political economy?

But, fortunately for the cause of truth, we are not confined to indirect deductions; and I shall bring before you a very striking circumstance, although, strange to say, scarcely, if at all, noticed by the superficial observer, but which to you, sir, must appear very extraordinary.

We find that the edition of Hume's History of England, to which I have just alluded, is prefaced by a biographical memoir of that infidel author, by the editor, who gives his own name in full, and foolishly fancies that he may acquire importance by styling himself the friend and admirer of the Scotch philosophist. He gives us a detailed account of the dying infidel, with a singular degree of self-importance. He represents him on the death-bed, and manifesting a worse than brutal obduracy of soul, in defiance to that God into *whose hands it is so terrible to fall unprepared!*

This officious friend informs us that Hume spent the time very comfortably in reading some amusing books. The *Dialogues of Lucian* were among the *last* and *religious* productions that occupied the attention of this *philosopher*, who inquired at the time what excuse he would give to old *Charon* for not going on board "the ferry-boat"! "I have endeavored," says he, "to open the eyes of the public; if I live a few years longer, I may have the satisfaction of seeing the downfall of some of the prevailing systems of superstition." He then cited a passage from *Chaulieu*, and on the 22d August, 1776, yielded up his infidel spirit.

Hereupon the editor of the work exclaims, "Thus died our excellent friend!" What can we think of a man who holds up the frightful death of such an individual to public admiration; who proclaims the sentiments of an atheist, and who, to his eternal infamy, prides in it? What are we to think of a *Christian* legislature, who received such a dedication, and to whom it never once occurred to require the slightest modification of the horrid preface? Above all, what idea can we form of the *spiritual* members of the House of Lords, on this *trying* occasion? People may speak as favorably as they please of *such* bishops, but they never will express all that they think of them. Without, however, disputing about the fact whether *such* prelates, like the *dumb dogs* of Isaiah, possessed any moral or pagan virtue, or not, I shall exclaim, in the words of Zaire, —

Genereux, bienfaisans, justes, pleins de vertus,
Dieu! s'ils etaient Chretiens, que seraient ils de plus!

Just, kind, and good, with every virtue crowned
In Christians, God! can higher gifts be found?

Neither can it be considered as deviating from the respect which is due to the legislature of France, when I state it as my deliberate conviction, that it contains a very large number of infidels who sprang into vicious existence during the late infamous, impious, and infernal revolution, and that there are even now in that national body by far too many who are mortal enemies to Christianity and regular government, while a decided majority of the members are more or less criminally indifferent to religion and the vital interests of the country. Notwithstanding this, I do believe that, were the two chambers solicited to accept a similar dedication, (we of course need not mention what the honest, Christian indignation of the respectable and venerable clergy and the king would be,) they would instantly spurn such an insult, so far at least as the insolent frontispiece was concerned.

Voltaire observed in 1766, and he repeated it in 1776, that " a few simpletons of Geneva still believed in consubstantiation ; as to the others, there was not to be found, from Berne to Geneva, a single individual who believed in Christianity!" He particularly and repeatedly stated that " the Christ would be disgraced in London."

Should any man, in the spirit of exaggeration, maintain that this hideous prophecy had been accomplished, and that the acceptance of so revolting a dedication was tantamount, on the part of the English legislature, and especially of the House of Lords spiritual, to an expressed and national renunciation of the Christian faith, he would be wrong; yet I should like to know how an honest and intelligent Englishman could invalidate such a conclusion!

This digression, sir, appeared to me to be of the utmost importance, because it shows that the English nation has no more right, and even less right, than any other country in the civilized world, to censure Spain for what has been misnamed her *detestable Inquisition;* and especially as that very institution has shielded her character from those *detestable* offences and nameless crimes of moral turpitude, which have characterized England for upwards of two centuries; from those *detestable* as well as deplorable calamities which have been the natural result of such conduct, and from the still more *detestable* and impious annihilation of religion, which exists only in name in that once great, but now oppressed, impoverished, and fallen "mistress of the deep."

In order to prove my positions, and point out the salutary effects of the INQUISITION, I have selected England in preference to any other country, because, unquestionably, even now, she holds the first rank among the Protestant nations of the earth, although, strictly speaking. there is not upon earth a truly Protestant nation. I have specified her because she possessed more ample means than any of her *kindred* countries to retain the faith, inasmuch as she adhered to a hierarchy and many useful forms; and yet she has completely sunk into such a state of perfect *indifferentism* that it would argue madness, *ultra toryism*, or the grossest stupidity, to contradict it. Contrast Spain with other Catholic countries, with France, for instance, or orthodox Germany, and you will be convinced that the Inquisition has served as a terrific and an impenetrable barrier against every kind of innovation which has so often not only torn asunder the strongest and dearest chords of society, but profaned what men and angels had for ages deemed most holy and pure.

To fulfil my promise, I shall not conclude this letter before I expressly declare to you that I am a mortal enemy to every kind of exaggeration, and am very far from weakening my cause by not wishing to make every due allowance for things. My object in writing these letters was to prove that the *Inquisition is, in itself, a salutary institution, which has rendered the most important services to Spain, and that it has been ridiculously and most shamefully calumniated by sectarian and sophistical fanaticism and falsehood.*

Here I stop. To suppose that I would sanction any abuse of any institution is out of the question. If the Inquisition has ever too strictly checked the daring enterprise of mind, committed any act of injustice, or displayed an excessive degree of suspicion, or security, (of all which I declare my perfect ignorance,) I shall be the very first to condemn whatever is censurable ; but I would never advise a nation to change her ancient institutions, which have been based upon the most cogent and prudential considerations, have been productive of such palpable advantages, and can scarcely ever be replaced by any so good. There is nothing under the influence and control of chance ; every thing exists for some cause. He who *pulls down* may be compared to an athletic child, who is at the same time a real object of compassion.*

---

* Let us even suppose that the Inquisition was characterized by deeds at once monstrous, cruel, and unnatural, and that even the Catholic hierarchy of Spain, — which we by no means admit, — lent their sanction to them, — what does all this prove ? Must the One, Holy, Roman, Catholic and Apostolic Church be held responsible for such conduct, and involved in one and the same promiscuous and damning imputation ? Such a conclusion would be a libel on logic and Christianity. — We are here so forcibly struck with the correct and appropriate passage contained in " Remarks, Analytical and Historical, &c. &c.," by the Rev. P. I. Carew, formerly professor of theology in the Royal Catholic College of Maynooth, that we deem an apology to the reader for its insertion quite unnecessary.

The reverend author of that pamphlet, showing up the absurdity of those who would fain impose the belief on themselves, or others, that the Catholic Church should be responsible for the opinions of every private theologian, and for the partial abuses of every age and country, expresses himself thus : " If it be absurd to impute to the civil legislature the positions supported by each writer on law, it is much more so to charge the Catholic Church with those advanced by unauthorized individuals of her communion.

" The obligation recognized by Catholics with regard to the doctrine to be believed, is complied with, if it be admitted that the promises of Christ to his Church have their accomplishment, when the lawful representatives of the apostles, in communion with the centre of Catholic unity, declare what is taught by the faith or morality of the gospel. For the peculiar opinions advocated by any of her members the Catholic Church is not accountable : they alone are individually responsible. If it be unjust to impute to the Catholic Church the peculiar opinions of individuals of her communion, it is equally so to charge her with the local abuses of any particular country. This will be at once evident, if we appeal to the words of Christ himself, and to the early history of the Church in the apostolic writings.

Whenever we reflect upon a great institution, or vast enterprise, which receives the sanction of nations, and especially of the *true Church* ; when, for instance, we view chivalry, the various religious establishments, such as the mendicant orders, instructors of youth, ascetics, missionaries, and knights hospitallers, as well as general indulgences, crusades, the Inquisition, and the like, we may unhesitatingly, as well as safely, concur in the sanction; and a cool, philosophical examination will soon recompense our confidence, by presenting us with a satisfactory demonstration of the great merits of each.

I have laid down an axiom in a former letter, and I shall here with my old friend Cicero, in one of his epistles, repeat it : "*Quid est quod contra vim sine vi fieri possit?* or, in other words, as you well know, *How can violence be repelled but by violence?* Nations would, in my opinion, best show their sense by not criticising or ridiculing each other's institutions:

That form of speech is frequent in the Scriptures, according to which his Church is called, by its divine Founder, the *kingdom of heaven*. Under this appellation, it is conveyed in the parable of the marriage feast, that the good and the bad may be members of it, and that a separation between them is to be effected only on the coming of the King. (1) The same truth is to be also learned from the parables of the wise and foolish virgins ; (2) of the net cast into the sea, (3) and taking in alike the good and the bad fish; of the field in which the tares are mixed with the wheat, to be separated only at the end, when the angels of God will gather the one into the barn, and cast the other into inextinguishable fire. (4) The doctrine contained in these parables is confirmed by the history of the particular churches founded in the apostolic times, and more especially by that of Corinth. Notwithstanding the partial abuses which, it appears from St. Paul, prevailed in the church of Corinth, the apostle continues to regard it as united to the society of the faithful, and is solicitous only to withdraw those guilty from their unhappy course, by enforcing the necessity of the virtues commanded by the gospel. Hence it is clearly deducible that objections against the Catholic Church, derived from the partial abuses that may have existed in particular places, are groundless and inconclusive." — *Translator.*

(1) St. Matthew, chap. 22.
(2) Idem, chap. 25.
(3) St. Matthew, chap. 13.
(4) Idem, chap. 13.

they should remember that they are not all placed in the same circumstances, and that certain emergencies will imperiously require of one to adopt particular measures, with which the others can dispense. Such, however, is the error, such the folly, of mankind. How common is it for men to exclaim against aged and useful institutions, and bring forward obsolete facts in order to upset them, after the time had elapsed, or the danger disappeared, wherein those institutions, or systems, were in themselves most wisely adapted to the state of things! How often does the mind sicken on reading the absurdities of legislative enactments for the restriction or suppression of certain authorities, which, on the contrary, ought to be protected and maintained by every possible means consistent with morality and religion!

The enemies of order and truth cite cases of the *auto da fe* of the sixteenth century, in order to pull down the Inquisition of the nineteenth; which is one of the mildest and wisest civil tribunals within the range of civilization. How obstinately do heretics and impolitic disorganizers declaim and fulminate their invectives against the power of the pontifical see!

We behold mankind acting under the influence of the curse of avarice, mistaken liberality, revolutionary *mania*, pride, and infidelity: they imagine that, by declaiming and writing against the power of the pope, they render immense service to the world; whereas, by their conduct, they not only foment the passions of depraved nature, and too frequently aim at self-aggrandizement, but powerfully contribute to their own destruction and that of civilization. Yes, where is the legislature or tribunal that is not already under arms to crush that power; at a time, too, when the world ought to know that the sovereign pontiff does not possess even the necessary means for the discharge of his immensely laborious and expensive functions? Even those college heroes and university champions who (as they supposed) have displayed such wondrous valor in wielding their pens against the pontifical power, which never did, and certainly does not now, terrify them, would, a few centuries ago, have kissed the very dust in the venerable presence of the supreme head of the Church. Yes, such would-be heroes have long exhibited *proofs* of their inconsistency. When nations submitted to the mild yoke of the cross, (and then there was more prosperity, honesty, honor, morality, and religion in the world,) when the piety of mankind poured, through the channels of charity, its streams of wealth into the reservoir of the Church, for the relief of indigence and the erection of temples to the living God, — where then were those doughty champions, with their restrictive measures and sumptuary laws? Were they not unnoticed and unknown? But when Infidelity, with her wicked and revolutionary train, walks abroad, — when desolating Tyranny has already swept into her unsanctified coffers the property of the widow, the orphan, the patriot, and the Church, — it is then, yes, and at this very moment, that we hear of such combatants rising up and concerting with "the great ones of the earth," to denude and disgrace the vicegerent of Christ, instead of contributing to enable him to impart *bodily* comfort to his flock, while, in compliance with the Savior's injunctions, *he feeds his lambs, and feeds his sheep*, with *spiritual* consolation and the *bread of eternal life.*

Thus is it that sovereignty is the constant dupe of innovation, and that nations fall into ruin, by vainly supposing that they have reached the climax of improvement, when they, in reality, become the vassals of selfish, ambitious, and unprincipled men.

Half of Europe must, forsooth, change its religion, in order to accommodate a profligate priest with a wife, or licentious princes with wealth; and such abominations must be hushed up, or palliated, under the plea that such things were indispensably necessary to counteract *Church abuses*, to commence a *reformation* in the Church of Christ, and present the world with *the pure word of God!!!!** Such *Protestant philanthropists* will, upon the same principle, swell the war-whoop against the *Inquisition*, while, in reality, the object of those *friends of humanity, liberty, science*, and *improvement*, is to obtain a patent for libertinism, and to speak, write, and do, what they please! The noble, rich, and worldly-wise of every class, who have to lose all, and gain nothing, by the demolition of social order, spell-bound, as they too frequently are, by those speculating and political sorcerers, enter into an unholy alliance with those whose great interest it is to upset it.

Strange infatuation! They become accomplices in a conspiracy which is levelled at themselves, and loudly advocate the cause of profligacy, under the specious name of *liberty*, which the wicked will invariably use for the execution of their nefarious designs.†

Such characters will rail at the whole code of penal laws, which have been enacted for their good, and will audaciously declare that they abhor even the shadow of the crimes which it is the intention of said laws to prevent. It would seem that a sensible

---

* Witness the wicked Cranmer, and his horrid master, Henry VIII.; the cruel Elizabeth, and the plundering duke of Somerset, the protector of Protestantism; Luther, and Philip, landgrave of Hesse-Cassel; and the thousands who feasted upon the *countless hecatombs* of the infidel revolution of unfortunate France. — *Translator.*

† The impious Voltaire and his confederate band (not forgetting Frederick of Prussia and the duke of Orleans, *Philippe Egalité*) were melancholy proofs of this assertion. — *Translator.*

man should actually witness such a moral delirium, before he could believe it; and, after all, he can never satisfactorily define it.

If other nations do not choose to establish the Inquisition, I am sure I have not the slightest objection. My only object in writing these letters is to justify Spain. I must, however, state that France in particular, without shutting her eyes against the light of reason, and steeling her heart against bitter experience, can never glory in having suppressed that institution. I will even add that, in any civilized and *Christian* nation, whatever tribunal is especially established for the prevention of crimes which particularly bear upon the morality and religion of a country, must *ever* be considered a highly-useful institution.

Finally, sir, it remains for me to make a remark upon another subject which has often occupied our minds. I mean, as you are aware, the acts of the present government of Spain. Our sentiments upon this point have been in perfect unison. We, at one time, could not conceive why the government adopted such stern and rigid measures; and we were accordingly tempted to pronounce them *shameful*, as England had thought proper to do. When we, on the other hand, reflected upon the natural kindness, and especially the great popularity, of the present king, we were inclined to believe that what is strictly called the Spanish nation is decidedly in his favor, and that his conduct is the direct result of his duty. In such a conflict of opinion, let us first see what is certain. In the famous manifesto of May 14, 1814, the king addressed his people to the following effect:—

"True and loyal Spaniards:
"Your hopes shall be crowned. It is for you alone

that your sovereign exists. Despotism I abhor and detest. Enlightened Europe cannot endure it; and to the glory of Spain be it said that her kings were ever averse to it. Although there have been times when the power of this nation was abused, and which no human institution could have completely prevented, yet to preclude their recurrence, as far as human wisdom can effect, by maintaining the unalienable dignity and rights of our crown and the inviolable rights of the people, I shall have an interview with your representatives of the two Spains and the Indies, and lay the deep foundation of my subjects' prosperity in a Cortes which shall be legally convoked. Personal liberty shall rest upon laws that will insure order and public tranquillity. The press shall be free, as far as sound reason will permit. Every prodigal waste of the national property shall cease, and the civil list expenditure shall be distinct from that of the government. In the enaction of all new laws, the sovereigns are to concert with the people. Upon such strong grounds you will ascertain my royal intentions, and be thereby enabled to regard me, not as a tyrant, or a despot, but as a king and a father," &c. &c. *

The university of Salamanca having been admitted to a solemn audience with the king, on the 13th of June, reminded him of all his promises concerning personal and real property, the liberty of the press, public appropriations, the reëstablishment of order,

---

* Yo os juro y prometto a vos ostros verdaderos y leales Espanoles .... Vuestro Soberano quiere serlo para vos ostros .... Aboresco y detesto el despotismo : ni las luces y cultura de las naciones de Europa lo sufren ya ; ni en Espana fueron depotas jamas sus Reyes.... Conservando el decoro de la dignidad real y sus derechos, pues los tiene de suyo, y los que pretenecen a los pueblos que son igualmente inviolables, yo trattare con sus procuradores, etc. etc. (Valencia, 4 mayo, 1814.)

and the convocation of the Cortes. The deputies of that great and illustrious body afterwards spoke to him to this effect: —

" Sire, — Your majesty has promised, and even voluntarily sworn, in your majesty's first decree, to terminate our calamities, and to establish the glory of Spanish royalty, by erecting on such a foundation the government of an heroical nation, who, by her immortal deeds, and the preservation of her honor and her liberty, has forced the world to admire her. Endless would be the efforts of the university, who view in unborn generations the happy consequences of these principles, were they to venture on a description of the gratitude and joy to which your majesty's intentions have kindly given birth. Your majesty remembers the representation which the Cortes, composed of the states ecclesiastic and noble, had forgotten; and your royal mind is perhaps still occupied with the reëstablishment of the ancient states, so as to give them that form which a wise policy has proclaimed to be best calculated, as far as man may expect, for a moderate and permanent government; and to consolidate for ages to come the equally inviolable laws of the monarch and the people," &c.*

Such, sir, is the language which the king had both expressed and heard. Did candor and honesty ever

---

* V. M. ha prometido y aun ha jurado espontaneamente en su primer decreto poner fin a nuestros males; colorando sus glorias en fundar sobre estas bases el gobierno de una nacion heroyca.... Pero la Universidad que ve mas de lejos las consecuencias de estos principios, no acaberia jamas si hubiesse de espresar toda su gratitud y su jubilo, etc., Recuerda (V. M.) la representacion olvidada en Cortes de los estados del clero y nobleza; y araso V. M. medita, etc. — 13 junio, 1814. (Gazeta de Madrid del Martes, 14 de junio de 1814, No. 85, p. 650.)

speak or act in so unequivocal a manner? Upon what grounds can such intentions of the king be suspected?

I shall not pass censure on those *questionable* acts which a stranger, and especially a foreigner, has no right to determine, much less to condemn. I feel thankful to the king for his promise; I rely upon his word, and am quite easy about the remainder. At all events, the abuses of ancient institutions can prove nothing against their essential merits, and I shall ever be of opinion that nations lose much, if not all, by tearing down their venerable establishments, instead of improving or repairing them. I shall feel extremely happy, sir, if these letters can remove any of your prejudices. You may, on a future day, return me a similar favor. Mankind frequently exchange errors; but, sir, it is the wish of my heart to open and perpetuate a far different kind of commerce with you. No mortification or failure can occur from so noble an exchange, where each party reserves the right to retain or commute. I shall conclude by saying that the minds of men may be compared to the earth, whose various qualities yield various fruits.

I am, &c. &c.

Moscow, Sept. 27, 1815.

FINIS.

THE BORROWER WILL BE CHARGED
THE COST OF OVERDUE NOTIFICATION
IF THIS BOOK IS NOT RETURNED TO
THE LIBRARY ON OR BEFORE THE LAST
DATE STAMPED BELOW.

Check Out More Titles From HardPress Classics Series In this collection we are offering thousands of classic and hard to find books. This series spans a vast array of subjects – so you are bound to find something of interest to enjoy reading and learning about.

Subjects:
Architecture
Art
Biography & Autobiography
Body, Mind &Spirit
Children & Young Adult
Dramas
Education
Fiction
History
Language Arts & Disciplines
Law
Literary Collections
Music
Poetry
Psychology
Science
…and many more.

Visit us at www.hardpress.net

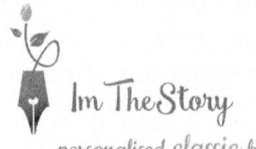

personalised classic books

"Beautiful gift.. lovely finish. My Niece loves it, so precious!"

Helen R Brumfieldon

★★★★★

UNIQUE GIFT

FOR KIDS, PARTNERS AND FRIENDS

Timeless books such as:

Alice in Wonderland • The Jungle Book • The Wonderful Wizard of Oz
Peter and Wendy • Robin Hood • The Prince and The Pauper
The Railway Children • Treasure Island • A Christmas Carol

Romeo and Juliet • Dracula

Visit **ImTheStory.com** and order yours today!

SD - #0034 - 130226 - C0 - 229/152/11 - PB - 9780371726273 - Gloss Lamination